Dan Kimball has done it again! Thoughtful. Provoking. Engaging. Liberating. A timely and much-needed celebration of church today. Highly recommended.

**Margaret Feinberg**, *www.margaretfeinberg.com*; author, *Scouting the Divine* and *The Sacred Echo*

Dan Kimball, more than any pastor I know, has found the heart, mind, and soul of the young adult of America. His book is insightful, pastorally warm, theologically sensitive. Dan's personal story, told honestly and gently, holds a mirror up to the church's subculture and unmasks it in order to heal the church and let it be what it really is—a place where messy people find God's good grace.

**Scot McKnight**, author, *The Jesus Creed* and *The King Jesus Gospel*

Dan's story hit close to home and challenged me immensely. Dan encourages us to break through the tension and messiness that church communities inevitably encounter to experience the beauty of being in community and sharing God's infinite love with others.

**Zach Lind**, drummer, Jimmy Eat World

Dan Kimball has approached a subject that may make some church folk uneasy, but the world is full of people looking for answers, real answers, and *Adventures in Churchland* is a great place to start looking for them.

**WS "Fluke" Holland**, drummer for Johnny Cash and Carl Perkins

Dan Kimball is the real deal. If you don't like the church, or if you're thinking about leaving, please read this book first. Dan's stories will make you laugh, make you think, and make you appreciate the church like never before.

**Mark Batterson**, author, *The Circle Maker*

Dan Kimball graciously reminds us that Christian community is a nonnegotiable element of discipleship and that we all contribute to making it a viable foretaste of the kingdom of God … or not.

**Alan Hirsch**, author; founder, Forge Mission Training Network

Dan's story of becoming a Christian is anything but preachy. It's warm, insightful, surprising, and often very funny. As a non-Christian, I was inspired and moved, and have been enthusiastically recommending it to my friends. This is a book for everybody.

**Mark Frauenfelder**, editor-in-chief, MAKE; founder, *boingboing.net*

Feel like you're disconnected from church? Read *Adventures in Churchland* from my good friend Dan Kimball. Dan will help you see that Jesus truly loves the church, despite the messiness of it. Dan provides hope on how we can be part of the church that truly reflects the gospel and makes a difference in the world.

**Brad Lomenick**, Catalyst Conferences

D1051954

I am so thankful for Dan Kimball. Here is a man who is real, honest, gritty, and compassionate. Dan loves the church not because he has to as a pastor, but because he wants to as a faithful follower of Christ. My friend has thought deeply on Scripture, church, and the world and is one of both culture's and Christianity's most needed voices and guides. This book is much needed.

**Britt Merrick**, pastor, Reality Santa Barbara; author, *Godspeed*

Being a Christian musician in a secular world is a unique opportunity. I related to Dan's story in this book both as a fellow drummer and believing it is an honor to represent God's love, peace, compassion, and kindness in the world. God's Word commands us to be the light of the world. I believe in the church we are able to shine our lights, and I have hope for the church doing this.

**Jessie Caraballo**, drummer for Marc Anthony

Dan Kimball encourages us not only to examine our own shortcomings but also to help us better understand that despite our many failures, God still wants to use us anyway. This book is a great read. One would be hard pressed to find another author who would weave Elvis, Johnny Cash, Wanda Jackson, and even Dee Dee Ramone into their writings as examples of the incredible fortitude of God's grace and mercy.

**Michael W. Stand**, guitarist and singer, Altar Billies (formerly of Altar Boys)

Dan does a great job of helping us navigate the questions and issues that so many of us face when it comes to dealing with the church and our relationship to it. Addressing hard questions and questioning the stereotypes, this book will help people understand how they can like Jesus and like the church as well.

**Rick McKinley**, Imago Dei Community; author, *Advent Conspiracy*

Dan Kimball gives us hope and inspiration to be the church that Jesus intended us to be.

**Jimmy VanEaton**, Sun Studio drummer for Jerry Lee Lewis,
Roy Orbison, and Billy Lee Riley

This one goes out to the skeptics and the seekers, the critics and the curious. For all those who want to believe in the church, but just can't seem to make it happen, this book is a must read.

**—John Mark Comer**, pastor, Solid Rock Church; author, *My Name Is Hope*

Over the years the church has developed a brand as an institution that "stands against" things. But what would happen if the church became known for what it stands for? Dan Kimball has once again brought fresh thinking to how beautiful the church can be. Read this book and together let's present the beauty of Jesus to the world.

**—Jake Smith Jr.**, Willow Creek Community Church

*Adventures in Churchland* challenged me to love the church and to see it as Christ does and as he longs for it to be.

**—Jason Ingram**, songwriter, producer, worship leader

# ADVENTURES
## IN
# CHURCHLAND

## FINDING JESUS IN THE
## MESS OF ORGANIZED RELIGION

FOREWORD BY WANDA JACKSON ★ MEMBER OF THE ROCK AND ROLL HALL OF FAME

# DAN KIMBALL

ZONDERVAN.com/
AUTHORTRACKER
*follow your favorite authors*

We want to hear from you. Please send your comments about this book to us in care of zreview@zondervan.com. Thank you.

ZONDERVAN

*Adventures in Churchland*
Copyright © 2012 by Dan Kimball

This title is also available as a Zondervan ebook.
Visit www.zondervan.com/ebooks.

This title is also available in a Zondervan audio edition.
Visit www.zondervan.fm.

Requests for information should be addressed to:

Zondervan, *Grand Rapids, Michigan 49530*

---

Library of Congress Cataloging-in-Publication Data

Kimball, Dan.
    Adventures in Churchland : discovering the beautiful mess Jesus loves / Dan Kimball.
      p. cm.
    Includes bibliographical references
    ISBN 978-0-310-27556-5 (softcover)
    1. Church. I. Title.
  BV601.7.K56 2012
  262—dc23                                     2011051667

---

All Scripture quotations, unless otherwise indicated, are taken from the Holy Bible, *New International Version®, NIV®*. Copyright © 1973, 1978, 1984, 2011 by Biblica, Inc.™ Used by permission. All rights reserved worldwide.

Scripture quotations marked TNIV are taken from the Holy Bible, *Today's New International Version™. TNIV®*. Copyright © 2001, 2005 by Biblica, Inc™. Used by permission of Zondervan. All rights reserved worldwide.

*Cover design: Rob Monacelli*
*Interior design: Matthew Van Zomeren*

*Printed in the United States of America*

---

12 13 14 15 16 17 18 /DCI/ 22 21 20 19 18 17 16 15 14 13 12 11 10 9 8 7 6 5 4 3 2 1

## THIS BOOK IS DEDICATED TO:

*Stuart Allen and Phil Comer*, two pastors who helped me see that not all Christians and churches are uncool, unintelligent, and mildly to majorly crazy, and who believed in me enough to spend time with me, put up with my hundreds of questions, and bring me into the mission of Jesus.

*The Altar Boys*, the Christian band that saved me from evangelical music weirdness.

*Becky, Katie, and Claire.* The book is finally done.

# ★ CONTENTS ★

## PART THREE

# GRACELAND

# ★ FOREWORD ★

**I AM SO GLAD THAT MY FRIEND DAN** has written this book, because there is a lot of confusion out there about Jesus and the church that needs to be cleared up. As Dan discovered in the adventures that he writes about, you might be surprised by what you find when you check out who Jesus is. There may be a whole lot more to walking with Jesus and living for him than you have realized or have been told. Despite all the great things I had happening in my life, for many years I was missing Jesus. I have toured with Elvis Presley, Johnny Cash, Jerry Lee Lewis, Buddy Holly, Adele, and so many other amazing musicians, but nothing compares to knowing Jesus.

I have learned that you can never really have the abundant and happy life you want until you know Jesus personally. But unlike what you might think, you don't have to give up a thing or change who you are to come to Jesus. You can come to him with all your hang-ups, confusion, and questions. And then, if there are changes that need to be made in your life, he will help you to make them. He will give you the strength you need to make the change. You don't have to do it before you come to him, and you don't have to do it alone.

My life was changed forever when I gave my heart and life to the Lord Jesus Christ. So wherever I go now, I can't help but want to tell other people about this. At every concert I perform, I take a few minutes to share about the wonderful difference Jesus has made in my life. As soon as I became a Christian, church was where I wanted to be. That's where I learned what it means to follow Jesus. I learned to pray and how to study the Bible. I also learned that churches are made up of people, so they will never be perfect. Yet as Dan writes in this book, Jesus *loves* the church, even when it is messy and imperfect.

I hope you will consider checking out who Jesus is and even being part of a church. I know that there are all sorts of stereotypes out there about the church and Christianity, and you may want nothing to do with that. I can't promise that your experience with the church and with other Christians will be perfect. But not all churches and Christians are like the ones that you may have heard about or experienced. My life has been changed by Jesus, and as you will read in this book, my friend Dan's life has been changed as well. And that's what I can promise you: that when you know Jesus personally and decide to follow him, your life will never be the same.

— Wanda Jackson, Queen of Rockabilly,
and Rock and Roll Hall of Fame Inductee
(*www.wandajackson.com*)

# ★ INTRODUCTION ★

## I LOVE THE CHURCH, DESPITE THE MESS

**I LOVE THE CHURCH.** If you knew the story of my life, you would never guess that I'd say that. You'd think it unlikely that I would be where I am today, dedicating my life to serving the local church and working with church leaders all around the world. Growing up outside of the Christian church, I always thought that the church was comprised of rather odd people. I believed that Christians didn't think for themselves but had their thinking dictated to them by their leaders, who held to a totally literal and inflexible interpretation of the Bible. I thought that most Christians were harmless, sincere, nice people, but were fairly naive to believe the things they believed, though I also had some experiences with Christians who weren't as nice — Christians who were judgmental, acted superior to others, and were often chauvinistic.

For the most part, I avoided the church and any interaction with Christians.

Occasionally, I had brief encounters with Christians, glimpses into the strange world of the evangelical Christian church, a place I refer to in this book as Churchland. In the chapters ahead, I will share some of my adventures in this world, stories of what it was like for me as an outsider looking in and the experiences that shaped my understanding of the Christian faith and of who Jesus is.

> **CHURCH·LAND:**
> *n.* The evangelical Christian subculture and all that goes with it, including music, language, codes of approval, and values.

## THE DILEMMA OF LIKING JESUS,
## BUT NOT THE CHURCH

Though today I am a Christian and belong to a church, that didn't happen overnight. I was quite resistant to Christianity. When I finally got to the point in my life where I was interested in exploring what the Bible and Christianity are all about, I experienced a strong sense of tension. The Christian church did not appeal to me. But I was intrigued by Jesus — who he claimed to be and what he said and did. The more I read about Jesus, the more I was fascinated by him, drawn to his teaching, even wanting to be like him. The more I learned about how Jesus loved people, how he cared for the poor, how he pointed out the hypocrisy of the religious leaders of his day, the more I grew interested in everything the Bible had to say about him.[1]

It was quite eye-opening for me to study the Bible for the first time, because before I actually read it, I had only a vague idea that Jesus had something to do with the Easter holiday, that he had come back to life somehow, but I had no understanding of the full story of the Bible leading up to his birth and why it was necessary for him to die on a Roman cross.[2] It all felt like a confusing series of fairy-tale stories. I was surprised when I learned the whole story line of the Bible and understood what the church is really supposed to be like.[3]

That's when my dilemma started. I was drawn to Jesus, but the Christians I had met and the churches I had experienced didn't seem too much like him. Therefore I didn't have much interest in associating with Christians, much less in becoming part of a church. But the more I learned about Jesus, the more I realized that Jesus himself seemed to suggest that the church, made up of his followers, is really important.[4] And the Bible says that Jesus is the "head" of the church[5] and tells us that the church is the "body" of Jesus here on earth.[6] Jesus created the church to be the community of his followers, those who are called to go into

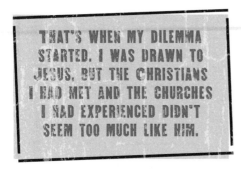

THAT'S WHEN MY DILEMMA STARTED. I WAS DRAWN TO JESUS, BUT THE CHRISTIANS I HAD MET AND THE CHURCHES I HAD EXPERIENCED DIDN'T SEEM TOO MUCH LIKE HIM.

the world on a mission to share God's love with those who do not know it.[7] The Bible tells us that Jesus loves the church, that he metaphorically thinks of his community of followers as his beautiful bride.[8]

Beautiful?

The church I knew and experienced didn't seem all that beautiful. I saw the church mainly as a mess of judgmentalism, dogma, contradiction, and hypocrisy. I thought about the Christian Crusades in the eleventh and twelfth centuries, when Christians used violence to force people to convert to their beliefs. And at least once a year, I saw a scandal in the news — yet another Christian leader getting caught doing the very thing he preached against. Then there were other Christians predicting the end of the world and then coming up with excuses when it didn't happen as predicted.

The church didn't seem too lovable to me.

## THE CHURCH IS MESSY BECAUSE WE ARE MESSY

I tried to stay away from the church because I didn't want to get involved in the messiness of it. After all, the church has done (and still does) some weird, embarrassing, and hurtful things. But I just couldn't escape the truth that the Jesus I saw in the Scriptures loves the church, despite the mess. And the reason is simple. Jesus loves the church because the church is made up of people. And Jesus loves people.

The real problem isn't the church. It's that people are messy. Every one of us. Like all people, Christians make mistakes. We sometimes say or do things that, intentionally or unintentionally, hurt people. We can be stubborn and have blind spots. The church is a community made up of messy people. Whether we are talking about a megachurch with thousands of people or a small house church meeting in a living room, since people are messy, the church will always be something of a mess.

A fascinating thing is that Jesus didn't choose a bunch of perfect people when he started his church two thousand years ago. His first followers weren't the religious superstars of his day.[9] Instead, Jesus chose ordinary, messed-up people to start his church. He chose people who made mistakes, many of which are recorded in the Bible for everyone to read.

Still, the fact that people aren't perfect doesn't mean we should give up and allow the messes we make to continue, never trying to change.

I have great hope that the church can become what Jesus wants it to be. In fact, I have dedicated my life to this hope of change. Though it is still a bit hard for me to believe, I came to a point in my life when I joined a church. Through a long process of study and prayer, I found myself believing in the church because Jesus believes in the church. Eventually I became a youth pastor and then started and led a new church with a group of people who shared a dream with me, a dream of a different kind of church that breaks down the stereotypes people believe about Christianity. I also began working with other leaders in churches around the country who want to see the church change.

This book is the product of another book I wrote called *They Like Jesus but Not the Church*,[10] an attempt to help leaders in the church understand some of the reasons why many people don't like the church and want nothing to do with Christianity, even though they are attracted to Jesus. I know many people who have had weird, strange, and even painful experiences with the church, experiences that left them disillusioned with and dismissive of Christianity. I wrote this book to offer them hope that there is more to the church and Christianity than they have seen or experienced. I wrote this book to encourage them not to give up on the church. I will be encouraging you to join in (if you haven't already) and be part of the change so that we can truly represent Jesus to the world with passion, integrity, humility, creativity, and love.

## WHAT LIES AHEAD

Because our experience of the church often profoundly shapes our understanding of the church, I'd like to begin by telling you my story. It's something of a journey, an adventure. Part 1 of this book is an introduction to the strange and unusual world of Churchland as I have experienced it, both as an outsider and now as a leader in the church. In part 2, I address two of the most common areas of tension and confusion I experienced as an outsider to Christianity encountering the culture of the church for the first time. Despite what I had read in the Bible, my personal experience reinforced many of my fears that the church is *judgmental* and that it's nothing more than *organized religion*. It took me some time to work through that confusion and understand that the church is more than this, that there is beauty in the mess. In part 3, I invite you to take a closer look at the church as Jesus envisioned it, what I refer to in this book as Graceland, and I share some ways that the church can change to become more like the church Jesus intended it to be.

If, after reading this book, you have questions that aren't addressed here, I encourage you to read a book that I wrote as a follow-up to this one, a book that dives into more of the objections and negative perceptions that people have of the church and their questions about its beliefs. That book is tentatively titled *Do You Like Jesus, but Not the Church? Exploring the Uncomfortable Questions about Christianity and the Church*. (See the epilogue for more information.)

As you read this book, I hope that this journey through Churchland and beyond it into Graceland will encourage you, challenge you, and most of all give you hope and understanding. I hope that you will come to see that the church is Jesus' plan for the world, and that despite the mess that Jesus' followers have often made, there is hope. If you have stories you'd like to share or comments you'd like to make about what you read in this book, you can find me online at *www.dankimball.com*. I'd love to hear your thoughts, questions, or points of disagreement, and I hope you

## IF YOU'RE READING
## THIS BOOK AS A GROUP:
Discussion questions for each chapter are available for downloading.

## IF YOU'RE USING
## THIS BOOK AS A CHURCH:
Helps and teaching outlines for pastors and leaders
are available for some of the content of this book.

Go to the Churchland book page on **www.dankimball.com**.

will share your hopes, stories, and dreams for the church with me. There will be a place for you to do that on the Churchland website in the "I dream of a church" section. There is exciting change happening out there in the church, and I look forward to *being* the change together.

*Note to the reader:* I refer to or quote lots of Bible verses in this book. I have put the references at the back of the book so you can look them up in a Bible or on the internet. (I used the New International Version [NIV] of the Bible.) Because this book is not written as a Bible study book, I don't go into the context of all of these Bible passages, but I can assure you that I have studied the context of every single verse I mention, and I encourage you to do the same.

## PART ONE

# CHURCHLAND

# CHAPTER ONE

# WELCOME
## — TO —
# CHURCHLAND

★ ★                    ★ ★

You may ask yourself, Well, how did I get here?...
You may ask yourself, Am I right, am I wrong?
You may say to yourself, My God, what have I done?
— *Talking Heads, "Once in a Lifetime"*

**CRAWLING ALONG THE FLOOR** on my hands and knees wearing a brown bedsheet, I was desperately trying to hide.

My God, how did I end up here?

Intensely embarrassed, I hid behind the fifty member choir, all of whom were wearing different colored bedsheets and blankets in their best attempts to imitate the style of New Testament times. They were standing onstage joyously singing music that was part opera, part Neil Diamond to a packed out room of around four hundred people in our church sanctuary.

It was our annual church Christmas musical, and I was supposed to be playing the role of a shepherd.

What made this such a bizarre moment for me was the fact that less than two years earlier, I was involved in a polar opposite type of musical experience playing drums in a punk and rocka-billy band in London. How did I get here? What happened to me?

## BEDSHEETS, BLANKETS, AND BAD MUSIC

If you've never been in a church musical before, let me give you a sense of what it's like. The shepherd costume I was wearing was sewn together from a chocolate-brown bedsheet, then secured around my waist with a belt of thick rope purchased at the hard-ware store. I also had a scarf to wear on my head and a thin, gold rope headband to tie it into place, but as soon as I saw myself with the gold headband, I felt so incredibly silly that I took it off. It looked like part of a children's pirate costume from Walmart, and I couldn't imagine that any respectable shepherd in Bethlehem would ever be caught wearing it.

I wasn't exactly a willing volunteer. I was in my midtwenties, and I was helping out in this church as a leader in the youth min-istry. One of the pastors in the church had decided that it would be good for the teenagers to see me — their leader — participating in the musical, and he'd strongly encouraged me to help out. Because I had not been raised in a church, the concept of a Christmas musi-cal was foreign to me, and the idea of being in one went against my better instincts, but I felt pressured to participate. Though I didn't understand how being in the Christmas musical would benefit the teenagers, I agreed to do whatever I could to help.

I didn't realize the extent of what I was getting myself into.

When rehearsals began, I started getting nervous. Listening to the music we were going to sing, I grew very uncomfortable. And the closer we got to the day of the performance, the more a feeling of dread settled in. Finally, I asked to be released from my commitment, but several people pressured me to stay, insisting yet again that it set a good example for the teenagers.

## SINGING CELINE DION SONGS TO BABY JESUS

We sang the contemporary evangelical choir music that was quite popular at the time. To me, someone who was fairly new to the world of the church, it all sounded like a collection of Michael Bublé or Michael Bolton love ballads, only not as good. I think the organizers of the event hoped this musical would somehow repli-cate the experience of a Broadway musical like *The Phantom of the Opera*. But that wasn't quite how it looked or sounded, although they tried their best. To this day, I have a vivid memory of the woman who played Mary staring intently into the face of Baby Jesus and then breaking out into a pop song, Celine Dion style.

To be fair, the choir did a really good job performing the songs that had been selected for them. I'm sure my grandmother in New Jersey would have enjoyed the music, and it might have even brought her to tears (in a good way). But by my personal standards, it was light years away from what I knew good music to be. Being associated with it went against everything I loved about music. It was like musical kryptonite. Listening to the songs made me feel weak, dizzy, and lightheaded. I know that musical taste is subjec-tive. But trust me, unless you were living in a retirement home, I am pretty sure you'd agree that the music wasn't something you'd listen to in your car stereo driving around town with your friends.

But it wasn't just the music or the costumes that caused me to hide behind the choir. It was also the presentation — the act-ing, the choreography. Everyone in the choir was encouraged to be overly expressive as we sang. We were told to extend our hands upward, all together, at the most dramatic moments in the songs. At other times, we were supposed to look frightened or happy or excited, and everyone did their best to perform in this melodra-matic style, moving about the stage as they sang.

I know that the choir members, most of whom were quite a bit older than me, were sincere in their desire to do their best, but we just weren't actors. I felt like I was surrounded by middle-aged aunts and uncles (and even some grandmas and grandpas) break-ing out into dramatized singing and waving their arms about. It was like they'd eaten too much Jell-O at the church picnic and were happily expressing the effects of the sugar rush.

## WHITE PLASTIC GARBAGE-BAG ANGELS

As odd as all of this was, it got even stranger when I saw the angel costumes. The angels wore white plastic robes, and when the lights hit them at the right angle, they even shined a bit. I think that may have been intentional. To me, though, it really looked like they were wearing oversized white kitchen garbage bags with their arms and legs poking out.[11]

Keep in mind that the people in the musical were kind and wonderful people. They had great motives. The musical was very meaningful to many of them. But it never would have crossed my mind to invite my non-Christian friends to something like this — unless we were grabbing a couple of drinks and heading to the musical for a fun night of odd and unusual entertainment.

## THE CONFUSION OF A MISFIT SHEPHERD

What finally led me to crawl around frantically on my hands and knees behind the choir that night was seeing all the people in the audience. During rehearsals, though I was nervous, I could excuse some of the more embarrassing elements of the musical. But at the performance, it felt entirely different. There were several hundred people looking up at the stage, watching me. As the music started up and we began singing our opening number, something just snapped inside of me. In a moment of rising panic, I thought, What in the world am I doing up here? What would my friends think if they saw me right now? What if someone I work with sees me up here and thinks I like this music? Oh, my God (and I really meant it when I thought "Oh, my God"), Why am I dressed in this chocolate-brown bedsheet?

So I ducked to the floor and hid behind the choir.

## PUNK-ROCKABILLY MEETS EVANGELICAL POP

What made this all the more of a bizarre, embarassing, frightening, and unreal experience was that music was everything to me. Just two years before, I was living in London, playing clubs and pubs as a drummer in a punk and rockabilly band. I loved music, especially the combination of punk and rockabilly we played. For years I was influenced by old-school big-band drummers like Gene Krupa and Buddy Rich, as well as jazz-rock drummer Danny Seraphine. But punk and rockabilly connected with me in a way that I couldn't shake. It was raw, emotional music that I deeply identified with.

Rockabilly is a musical style that developed in the early 1950s, going against the grain of the safe popular music of the day. Rockabilly is an experimental fusing of rhythm and blues — the type of music you could hear on Beale Street in Memphis — with country and western. Sam Phillips, who ran Sun Studio in Memphis, was a pioneer of this genre, and he discovered and recorded classic rockabilly musicians like Elvis Presley, Carl Perkins, Johnny Cash, and Jerry Lee Lewis. Other musicians and bands like the Johnny Burnette Trio, Little Richard, Wanda Jackson, Gene Vincent, Bo Diddley, Eddie Cochran, and Chuck Berry are also early examples of this style, and they were my musical heroes.[12] They were innovators in both music and fashion, fusing different styles to create a style distinct from the popular culture of the time.

In a similar way, punk music rebelled against the mainstream, the popular music of the 1970s. Punk music stripped down the bloated beast of disco and arena rock to something raw, emphasizing the garage-band roots of many of its musicians. Bands like The Clash, The Ramones, the Sex Pistols, and the band X from Los Angeles broke new musical ground, shocking some people but resonating with others. Topper Headon from The Clash, D. J. Bonebrake from X, and Bill Bateman from The Blasters were drummers I carefully watched and tried to imitate musically.

Not only did I love the music, but I loved the fashion and the personal expression of the musicians who played these musical genres. Both rockabilly and punk musicians pioneered unique clothing and unusual hairstyles. I tried to imitate the pompadour hairstyle of the early rockabilly artists, as well as their clothing. Aesthetics and art were important to many of the punk bands and their music. Two members of The Clash attended art school in England before forming their band. The Ramones and the Sex Pistols had a thoughtful, deliberate approach to what they wore, crafting the image they presented to the public. This was the musical scene that I lived in.

Musically and culturally, the world of the evangelical church choir was the antithesis of everything I loved.

## BACK TO THE MUSICAL

Crouched behind the choir, I felt trapped. Blood rushed to my head, and I began hyperventilating a little. When several choir members moved to the front of the stage, I crawled across the floor on my hands and knees like a frightened little monkey to avoid being seen.

Somehow I managed to stay hidden.

For the entire musical.

Although the program lasted only an hour, it felt like an eternity before the choir sang the final dramatic note, raising their arms high in the air in choreographed unity. The lights went out. The people applauded. It was finally over.

As the choir moved offstage, I stood up and walked out with them, acting as though I'd been there the entire time. I ducked out the side door of the church building and walked to my car, still wearing the brown sheet over my clothing. I skipped the reception and drove straight home.

And I never sang in a church musical again.

# CHAPTER TWO

# CHURCHLAND, THE MUSICAL

★ ★ ★ ★

Why am I such a misfit?
I am not just a nit wit!...
Why don't I fit in?

— *"We're a Couple of Misfits," from
Rudolph the Red-Nosed Reindeer*

**DO YOU REMEMBER** that classic stop-motion animation Christmas movie *Rudolph the Red-Nosed Reindeer*? The story begins with the preparations for Christmas at the North Pole. Everyone is anticipating the special day with excitement, everyone except a reindeer named Rudolph and his elf-friend, Hermey, who just don't feel like they fit in. They decide to run away from home and, in wonderful cartoon fashion, sing a song lamenting that they feel like nothing but a couple of misfits.

As someone entering the world of Churchland, I could very much relate to Rudolph and Hermey. I felt like a misfit, like someone who didn't fit the status quo of the church. My experience in the Christmas musical was just the beginning of an adventure, a process of learning to live in a culture that felt extremely foreign to me.

I now realize that not all church musicals are bad or embarrassing. Some are creatively written and professionally performed. And I recognize that even when the quality is bad by artistic standards, the people who put on these performances are doing it because they love God. They just want to tell the biblical story of the birth of Jesus or celebrate the story of the resurrection at Easter.[13] Many churches use musicals or performances like this every year, and really there is nothing wrong with that.

My point is not to bash church musicals. It's to illustrate the fact that there are many things Christians do — with good intentions — that can be quite embarrassing or confusing to others. Sometimes even other Christians have trouble understanding why Churchland is the way it is. Many Christians today feel like an outcast or a misfit within their own churches and may be embarrassed to say that they are Christians, not because they are ashamed of Jesus but because they don't agree with many of the things that other Christians say or do that have nothing to do with Jesus.

My experience with the church musical is a metaphor I use to describe my entry into the organized church. At the time, I wanted to hide from people because I didn't want to be associated with the music and the style of the church musical. But since then, I have sometimes wanted to hide my identity as a Christian, not wanting to be associated with the cultural baggage of the church. I've found that my earliest encounters with the church contain some insights that can help us better understand the strange and unusual world of Churchland.

## "WHY AM I SUCH A MISFIT?"

**1. People may feel like misfits in the church not because they dislike Jesus but because they don't fit in with Churchland culture.**

One of the most confusing things for me, being in the Christmas musical, was seeing how excited everyone else was about what we were doing. During the rehearsals, several people said to me, "Dan, isn't this going to be a great musical?" "This is such a wonderful song!" And I nodded and kept quiet. Maybe they're right, I thought. I was just trying to fit into this new church community and understand my new role serving in the youth ministry.

Maybe, I thought, this is music that Jesus would like if he were walking around today. Perhaps the other choir members know better than I do.

© 1964 Rankin/Bass Productions/Rick Gold-schmidt Archives, www.miserbros.com

At that time, I didn't real-ize that there are traditions, beliefs, and ways of doing things in the church that have nothing to do with the Bible or the teachings of Jesus. Now, as a leader in the church, I know firsthand that often what many churches do is a reflection of a specific church culture influenced by a denomination or the history of that church. But at first, I naively assumed that anything a church does is what the Bible teaches and is representative of Christianity. I felt there was something wrong with me if I didn't like a particular musical style or the way a worship gathering was designed.

## 2. The church sometimes presents a weird and confusing expression of the Christian faith, particularly to those outside Churchland.

Besides musical styles, other things can leave people who are new to the faith or investigating Jesus feeling disconnected, such as a church's approach to leadership or preaching, or its language or unwritten dress code or unspoken rules of conduct. These things may have nothing to do with the Bible, but they have become part of how things are done at the church. They may have been doing these things for years, no longer questioning why. They may not even real-ize they have cultural codes. But a church's unwritten rules and cul-ture are the first things people outside the church notice, and they shape people's understanding of Christianity. In many cases, aspects of a church culture come across as weird, confusing, and strange.

In the Christian church, musicals like the one I was involved in happen each year. But as a relatively new Christian, this inner world of Churchland was not my land, and it wasn't a place any of my friends had ever visited either. Participating in this musical was like stepping into an entirely different culture. Though most of the people in the choir were people I would have totally loved to introduce to my friends, the cultural oddities of Churchland would have been the biggest stumbling blocks to introducing my friends to my new church community.

But what worried me about the musical wasn't just the costumes, the music, or the people in our church. I worried about the message we were communicating.

**3. In Churchland, we sometimes skip the difficult questions and avoid digging into our faith, making those who ask questions feel uncomfortable.**

Because I wasn't raised in the church, it wasn't until my college years that I started reading the Bible. When I did read the Bible, I had so many questions I was forced to get below the surface and dig as deeply into it as possible. Everything was different, and I was reading the Bible with fresh eyes. I had studied the account of Jesus' birth, so after seeing how the musical presented the Christmas story, I sensed that something was amiss. I knew that the musical wasn't entirely accurate.

Unlike the intense and drama-filled story of Jesus' birth as told in the Bible, the presentation felt more like a Disney fairy tale. It was a really nice story meant to inspire uplifting emotions, similar to how you might feel when watching Snow White awaken from her deep sleep after being kissed by Prince Charming. But I noticed that there were significant differences between the way the church musical presented the Christmas story and what I read in the Bible.

For example, seeing Mary and Joseph break forth into a joyful, choreographed duet at the announcement of Jesus' birth is a bit of a departure from reality. In the biblical narrative, Mary does sing or recite a poem.[14] But I'm quite certain it wasn't while dancing with Joseph. Instead, the couple most likely went through some trying times, explaining to the community how Mary, as a virgin, had gotten pregnant. Mary's reputation — even her very life — would have been at stake. She could have been stoned to death for being found pregnant while promised to Joseph before their wedding. We catch a glimpse of Joseph's reaction and sense the embarrassment and betrayal he must have felt until he, too, received a message from an angel, telling him the truth about Mary's pregnancy.[15] It must have been a challenging time for the couple, their friends, and their families as they wrestled with the news that Mary was pregnant. These were real people, and like any of us, they must have felt angst and embarrassment as their lives were disrupted by the announcement that Jesus would be born. But the tension and fear of Mary and Joseph's experience wasn't shown in the musical.

Nor did the musical explain the context of Jesus' birth: the biblical understanding of the kingdom of God, why the Roman government was a major player in the events that unfolded. The musical version of the story skipped the horror of the slaughter of male children under the age of two in Bethlehem, an act ordered by the government ruler, King Herod.[16] These are all essential parts of the Christmas story, but the musical focused more on the nostalgic images that we see on Christmas cards: the star shining down on an incandescent Baby Jesus on a quiet winter night, surrounded by singing angels and nice clean animals looking at him in a choreographed pose.

I don't mean to upset your image of the Christmas story. It was a miraculous night that truly did bring amazing joy to the world.[17] Jesus, the Savior, was born. What greater joy can we have than this? But the Christmas musical reminds me that we can sometimes present people with a sanitized version of the Bible, focusing on the parts we like the most, while ignoring parts we don't like or don't understand. We even portray some of the story inaccurately. The toughest part for me to understand at that time was that no one seemd to question it.

For instance, it likely wasn't a barn but a cave that Jesus was born in, a cave under a home, a place where the animals were stored. Jesus probably was laid in a dirty stone feeding trough, which was the manger. And I'm sure he cried, like all babies do. But the baby in the musical didn't cry. He lay angelically on the stage in a perfectly clean and freshly built wooden manger lit in a magical glow by the spotlight.

I suppose the special lighting on the baby was to represent the star that the three kings followed, wearing crowns and bringing gifts to Jesus in the manger. But that misrepresents the biblical story too. Jesus was not visited by these special guests until anywhere from several weeks to two years later. The Bible clearly says that Jesus was in a house when they presented their gifts to him, not at the birthplace in a cave.[18] And they weren't even kings. They were magi, non-Jewish religious astrologers who, from astronomical observations, had inferred the birth of a great Jewish king. They came to Bethlehem to see the child king they believed was being born. The magi may have been from Arabia, Babylon, or somewhere else — we don't know for certain.[19] And it's likely there weren't even three of them. The idea that there were three kings visiting Jesus in the manger comes from a Christmas carol, "We Three Kings," written around 1860 by a pastor in Pennsylvania. And even the star is not mentioned in the Bible as being visible on the night of his birth. The star — or whatever it was that guided the magi — doesn't show up until later in the story when the magi visited Jesus. There is no mention of the star in the manger scene.

Even the date we use today, December 25, was not actually the day of Jesus' birth. Shepherds, in all likelihood, weren't out in the fields during the winter months, so many scholars think that Jesus was born in the spring, not on December 25. In the third century, church leaders selected December 25 as the date for Christmas to counter a holiday celebrating the birthdays of various pagan gods. The Persian god Mithra, the Greek god Dionysus, and the Egyptian god Osiris all had birthday celebrations on that date, celebrations tied to the winter solstice. Since no one knew the actual date of Jesus' birth, the church felt that celebrating Jesus' birth on that day would steer attention away from those pagan gods.

I can totally understand using artistic license to present a story. And I know that musicals are not meant to replace in-depth study of the Bible. Even so, I wondered why I never heard any of the people in our church asking questions about the differences between the church musical version and the biblical account. I did eventually ask one church leader about the questions I had, and it turned out he didn't know that December 25 was not the actual date of Jesus' birth. He even unintentionally made me feel like it was silly to ask about the actual date of Jesus' birth, as well as to raise the other questions I had. This church leader likely would feel terrible if he knew he made me feel that way, but when I asked sincere questions about the biblical account of Christmas, he brushed them off. I understand that we don't want to focus on trivial things, but this got me thinking. Isn't asking questions a good thing? And shouldn't we really be studying what we believe beneath the surface level? If we get parts of the Christmas story wrong when we present it, what else do we get wrong?

The Bible is a book filled with tension and difficult passages. But I have observed that in Churchland, we tend to ignore the difficult parts of the Bible and sometimes even "Disney-fy" our Bible stories, giving them happy endings that teach moral lessons, frequently sacrificing accuracy and avoiding the tough questions of faith.

As far as I was aware, I was the only one with these concerns. At that time, I felt quite alone in my questions and like a misfit. I now realize that I wasn't alone and that so many others also have questions and sometimes feel like misfits in the church. So if you have ever felt like a misfit, know that you're not the only one.

## HOPE FOR THE CHURCH

As I look back on my experience in the Christmas musical, I actually am quite thankful for it. It awakened me to the evangelical subculture of the church, the world of Churchland, and forced me to take a hard look at what I was getting involved in. My concerns went far beyond the musical style and the costumes. I began thinking about the church: what really makes the church the church. I began to wonder why churches do what they do and where they got their ideas, what informed their theology.

I share this story with you because it represents a defining moment in my life and in my understanding of the church and its relationship to the world. I was a young misfit looking for a place to call home, and I easily could have lost my trust in "organized religion." I could have given up and abandoned the church.

But I ended up staying in that very church, despite what I felt was embarrassing music and the bedsheet costumes. That same church went on to become a major source of joy in my life. It was the church that first gave me an opportunity to serve in ministry, and eventually I was hired as a staff member. God used that church to shape and refine me in many wonderful ways, teaching me and deepening my understanding of what it means to follow Jesus. For sure there were some confusing and difficult moments, and I almost gave up on church. But I didn't, and my life has never been the same. I'm so incredibly thankful I didn't give up.

Many people today want nothing to do with the church. Many people don't trust church leaders. Many feel as if the church and the Christian faith are only for the dogmatic and closed-minded.

They believe that true spirituality isn't about doctrines or even personal beliefs; it's about acts of love. And when they look at Christian churches, they don't see love; they see only fear and division. Perhaps they have tried church but have not found it to be a safe place for asking their questions. Some have experienced judgment or criticism and even have been wounded by the church.

For those of you who aren't Christians, and for those Christians who have had negative experiences with the church, I understand how weird the church can sometimes seem. I admit that the church started by Jesus has done some pretty horrible and unusual things throughout history. But there is also something wonderful about the church, a beauty that many people don't get to see and often remains hidden from the world. Despite the sometimes bad music, bedsheets, and angels in white garbage bags, the church isn't really as crazy as you might think. If your impressions of the church are formed by limited interactions with Christians or from reports in the news, you've likely experienced the loudest voices, voices that are frequently extreme in their views and that have understandably colored your impressions of the Christian faith and of the institutional church. I want you to know that not all who claim to follow Jesus agree with these voices, and most Christians are not like the extreme ones you may have experienced.

But I wouldn't be writing this book if I didn't have hope for the church. Yes, there are lots of valid criticisms of Christians and the church. Many Christians even agree with those criticisms and want to see things change, and they are working to make those changes happen in their local churches. We're tired of being known as a judgmental, homophobic, chauvinist, fundamentalist, organized religion that puts out bad music and bad movies. And we really want to change that.

I'm writing this book as one of many voices proclaiming that there is hope to be found *in* the church, and that the church can change and become the community that Jesus intended it to be. I'm writing this book to give hope to the misfits who feel like foreigners in Churchland. And I am writing for those of you who have never set foot in a church, to help you gain some insight into the strange world of evangelical Christianity.

I'll start with my own story.

# CHAPTER THREE

# I WOULDN'T LIKE CHRISTIANS IF I WEREN'T ONE

★ ★ ★ ★

> Christians are hard to tolerate. I don't know how Jesus does it.
> — *Bono*

**HONESTLY**, if I weren't already a Christian, I don't think I actually would like Christians. If I hadn't been involved with several wonderful churches and interacted with Christians who lived the way Jesus taught his followers to live, I'd naturally form my perceptions about Christianity from the perspective of an outsider.

For most of my youth, that's exactly what happened.

It's not as if I decided one day that I wasn't going to like Christians. It just so happened that the Christians I encountered were not people that I could identify with. Whether it was their personality, style of clothing, the way they presented themselves, or what

I saw on televsion about them, I just wasn't drawn to the church or Christianity.

## MY FIRST ENCOUNTER WITH AN EVANGELICAL CHRISTIAN

I was born and raised in northeastern New Jersey, near New York City. New Jersey was a wonderfully weird place to grow up. I lived somewhere near the place where they filmed the HBO television series *The Sopranos*. My New Jersey soundtrack growing up was Bruce Springsteen songs, and John Travolta and Tom Cruise went to high school in nearby towns. My suburban town was a place where *Seinfeld* met Sylvester Stallone's *Rocky*, with a bit of *Saturday Night Fever* thrown in. Strangely enough, the people in these fictional stories are pretty similar to the people I grew up with.

My family weren't churchgoers, and I didn't spend any time seriously thinking about religion or God. I had just a few church experiences, times when my parents took us to a church, dropped us off, and then picked us up again. It was a church whose building was built in 1725, and George Washington went there a few times, which was highlighted a lot in that church. I came out of there thinking that George Washington was somehow part of the Bible it was mentioned so often. Both of my parents later became Christians, which was a wonderful thing. But none of those church experiences really introduced me to Jesus. It wasn't until I had my first encounter with an evangelical Christian at the Paramus Park shopping mall that I was challenged to really think about Jesus and what he had done.

I was in eighth grade. My friend Ralph and I were hanging out at the mall, as most junior highers do. Since we'd soon be freshmen, we were trying to find some high school girls to talk to. We figured that if we wore our KISS and Led Zeppelin[20] T-shirts, a high school girl might see us and want to talk to us.

Not a single female, of any age, even gave us so much as a glance. While we were standing around the waterfall in the mall, awkwardly trying to look cool, a guy in his midtwenties walked up to us. He looked like some sort of hippy, with his hair past shoulder length, and he was wearing a tan suede jacket with fringe like

Daniel Boone's. He just walked up to us and, without even saying hello, asked, "Do you know Jesus?"

We were caught quite off guard. If you think about it, that's an odd question to start a conversation with, especially if you're dressed like Daniel Boone. But since talking to someone helped us feel less like failures, even though we couldn't attract any female attention, we talked to this fellow. Looking back, I understand that he was evangelizing us, but at the time I didn't have a clue what he was doing.

As you might imagine, we had no idea how to answer his question, and we squirmed uncomfortably, standing there in awkward silence with blank looks on our faces. I knew that Jesus had some relation to God and that he had something to do with Easter a really long time ago. But this guy had asked us if we *knew* Jesus, like we might be friends with Jesus or knew where he lived and planned to hang out with him that afternoon. It was sort of like someone asking me if I knew Abraham Lincoln or another figure from the past.

We continued to waffle, so he asked, "Do you know if you are going to heaven or hell?" We had only just met this guy, and here we were talking with him about our inevitable deaths. We were eighth graders in a shopping mall, dealing with identity and self-esteem issues, worried about blemishes, puberty, and meeting girls. We weren't standing around pondering whether we were going to heaven or hell.

When we couldn't muster an answer to either of his questions, he pulled out a little Bible from his backpack and opened to some pages, pointing out verses he had underlined in colored pencil. They were all about being thrown into a lake of fire if your name wasn't written in some book. He read about how we would be tormented for all eternity. He read a line from the Bible, paused, and then looked us straight in the eye to communicate the seriousness of what he was saying. Then he read another line, working through several passages about hell, fire, the devil, demons, and eternal damnation.

Now, hearing an adult tell us all of this in such a serious manner was absolutely terrifying. It was totally freaking our junior high minds out. We became fixated on every word as he read several more horrifying Bible verses. I don't remember all that he read or shared with us, but he kept telling us that Jesus died, and that because he died, we could avoid hell and all the terrible things we were hearing.

Finally, he stopped reading and asked, "Do you want to pray, so you don't get thrown into the lake of fire?"

We didn't have to think about that one too long. We knew that we didn't want to be thrown into any fiery lake.

Looking back on this, my first encounter with an evangelical Christian, it's really freaky to think we did all this with a stranger, but we followed him out into the parking lot of the Paramus Park mall to a grassy parking median. We knelt in the grass with him and repeated some words he told us to say. I now know it was the classic Sinner's Prayer used by evangelists for praying with someone to become a Christian. At the time, all my junior high mind could think was, "I don't want to go into the lake of fire. I don't want to go into the lake of fire. Please don't send me into that lake of fire."

I remember thinking, though, as we knelt to pray, that I didn't care if anyone saw me. I was as self-conscious as any junior high student, but for the few moments we were kneeling there on the grassy median, it just felt right to pray that prayer. I figured that the embarrassment of being seen kneeling in the grass and praying was nothing compared with the torment of the lake of fire I'd just heard about. So I repeated the words we were told to pray.

And that was it.

## YOU'RE NOW SAVED. HERE'S A STICKER. GOODBYE!

Afterward, it was a little awkward. Maybe more than a little awkward. I had no idea what to think or say, so I was just quiet. We got up from our kneeling positions, and Daniel Boone told us that we were now saved. Then he shook our hands quite firmly and smiled with the pride of someone who has just conquered something. He reached into his backpack and gave us each a little round sticker that said, "I found Jesus." After a quick goodbye, he dashed off into the parking lot, like a superhero disappearing after an amazing rescue. He left us standing there in the grass wondering what had just happened, holding tightly to our "I found Jesus" stickers.

With nothing better to do, Ralph and I walked back into the

mall, and finding no girls to flirt with, we headed home. We didn't say a word about what had just happened. It was such a strange experience that I don't think either one of us knew what to think. If it weren't for the stickers in our hands, it would have been easy to believe it was all just a dream.

The only time Ralph and I ever talked about what happened was the next morning at school. I awkwardly asked Ralph what he thought about our experience at the mall. He sheepishly looked down, muttered "I don't know," and that was that the end of it. We never talked about it again. I was always a bit unsettled by the

## "THE FEAR OF THE LORD IS THE BEGINNING OF WISDOM" —PSALM 111:10

I do believe that the Bible teaches that there is a hell. But I don't believe that scaring junior highers you don't even know with threats of hell and lakes of burning fire is the best way to introduce them to Jesus. It was quite confusing to sort through later on. I can say, however, that the tactic did give me something of a jolt—a sense of holy fear and reverence and the beginning of an awareness that there might actually be consequences to the choices I was making in my life. As strange as this encounter was for a junior high student, it did get me thinking. As I got older and entered my college years, that seed of reverence for God led me to ask a lot of questions.

In the Hebrew Bible,[21] particularly in the books of Psalms and Proverbs, several passages speak about the fear of God. Not a cringing, scary sort of fear like you experience watching a slasher film, but a *holy* fear, the realization that God is real and that there is no one and nothing as incredible, awesome, and amazing as God. The Bible often reminds us to start our thinking about God from the right perspective—that we are created beings and that God is the Creator of all things.[22] Knowing who we are in relationship to our Creator should instill in us a holy fear, a sense of reverence and respect for God. We learn to recognize that our lives are not, ultimately, under our control and that one day we will die and, as the saying goes, meet our Maker. This sense of reverence leads us to seek God. When we understand who we are in relationship to God, we then naturally desire to seek his wisdom and knowledge, as several scriptural passages suggest.[23]

whole thing. After all, why would an adult stranger dressed like Daniel Boone walk up to a couple of thirteen-year-olds and read Bible verses to them, telling them that they were possibly going to be thrown into a lake of fire? I had never known anyone who did that sort of thing. I'm willing to allow that our mall evangelist had sincere motives, and that he really, truly wanted us to avoid going to hell, but still, it's a pretty weird thing to do if you stop to think about it.

## BRAM STOKER'S *DRACULA*, THE LORD OF THE RINGS, AND THE HOLY BIBLE

As the years passed, I kept that encounter with the Daniel Boone evangelist in the back of my mind and sometimes wondered about that prayer I said. I tried reading a Bible that my parents gave me, but I could not make any sense of it. It seemed like a medical dictionary to me, with words and names that were hard to pronounce. Still, I sensed that it was a special book, so I placed it on the bookshelf in my room, right between my J. R. R. Tolkien *Lord of the Rings* paperbacks and a copy of Bram Stoker's *Dracula*. It seemed to fit well there as an adventurous, somewhat spooky book. But during high school, I gave up trying to read it on my own.

It wasn't until I attended Colorado State University that I had another serious encounter with evangelical Christians. Even though I wasn't a Christian, I respected God. But I still didn't understand the whole organized religion thing. I tried again, unsuccessfully, to read the Bible. Whenever I read it, it was so strange and difficult to understand (especially because I began reading in the Hebrew Bible). It also didn't really seem to make any difference in my day-to-day life. I was having fun as a college student, enjoying life, and had begun playing in a punk-rockabilly band. Music had become a major part of my life.

Yet throughout that time, I wondered, often late at night when I was about to fall asleep, about that prayer I had said outside the Paramus Park mall long ago. What did it really mean? What did it mean to be saved? Who is God? Is there really a hell and a lake of fire? In my late-night ponderings, I often wondered if my interest in Christianity was simply the product of living in America. What if I had, instead, been born in India? Would I be asking questions about Islam or Hinduism instead of Christianity? What if I had been born in China? Would I be a Buddhist? I was becoming increasingly aware of the various world faiths, and learning that Christianity was by no means the only religion to consider.

No one prompted me to ask these questions. I didn't have Christian friends trying to persuade me to join them. It just seemed impossible to me *not* to wonder whether God is real, to question what Christianity is really all about, and to be confused about why there are so many religions in the world.

## CHRISTIANS = SHINY HAPPY PEOPLE HOLDING HANDS

One day, I read in the school newspaper that every Wednesday night, many of the Christian college students gathered together on campus. Curious about Christianity, I thought I'd give one of their meetings a try. I went by myself, not telling any of my friends where I was going. I felt it would have been awkward if I told them I was thinking of going to a Christian meeting. As I neared the doorway, I could hear music and clapping coming from the room. Very cautiously, I peeked through the door at the rear of a large classroom. Immediately, I was overwhelmed by a great sea of pastel colors. The vast majority of people in the room wore something white, pink, light blue, or aqua green. I felt like I was peering into a *Miami Vice* fan club meeting.[24] I was wearing my black leather jacket and my usual rockabilly wardrobe, and I felt very out of place. Even as my fashion sensibility reeled from pastel shock, I was equally jolted by the music. I didn't recognize any of the songs they were playing, but they were quite peppy and upbeat, and everyone was clapping and singing along. I'd never heard any contemporary Christian worship music before, but it reminded me of commercial jingles or the theme song to a TV sitcom like *The Brady Bunch*. But I watched the scene before me with a mixture of horror and astonishment and was almost hypnotized by all the happy clapping to the beat that was going on.

I had never seen anything like this before.

The speaker stood up (wearing a pink golf shirt), and I was struck by how incredibly cheery he was, smiling constantly as he talked. As I listened, I heard a lot of unfamiliar phrases, Christian lingo and rhetoric that I didn't understand. Everyone else knew what he was saying, though, responding with shouts and clapping during parts of his message. Standing in the back, I scanned the room, looking for someone I could relate to, but all I could see were these happy clapping people everywhere. I just knew that there was no way I could relate to the people at this meeting — the music, the clapping, the singing, the pastels, and above all else that overly cheery disposition everyone seemed to have.

Please understand that I know that these types of judgments about music and fashion are trite and surface level. I know that it's wrong to jump to conclusions, but the fact remains that's what I did when I was a college student, and this experience shaped my understanding of Christianity at the time. I wasn't really interested in looking past the outside to see the inner reality of what was happening. All I knew was that I had visited this Christian meeting and it felt very strange. I understand now that this group of Christians wasn't *always* happy-clappy, but the vibe I got from the meeting was enough to make me want to quickly get out of that place as fast as I could. I felt like I had intruded on some strange tribal rite that I wasn't supposed to see. Eventually, someone noticed me leaning against the rear wall and began walking over to me, extending his hand to greet me. But I panicked and fled from the classroom.

Shiny happy people holding hands
Shiny happy people laughing

There's no time to cry
Happy, happy
Put it in your heart
Where tomorrow shines
Gold and silver shine

— REM, "Shiny Happy People"[25]

The REM song "Shiny Happy People" describes what I felt about this group of Christians: a harmless group of people, odd, somewhat goofy, overly cheery, and definitely not in touch with the culture around them. They seemed like nice people who didn't bother anyone, and if they minded their own business, they wouldn't cause anyone harm. This experience led me to believe that Christians are happy-clappy, somewhat-goofy people who like to sing and smile a lot.

## CHRISTIANS = WHISPERING PEOPLE DOING STRANGE RITUALS ON ORANGE CARPETS

I felt that I wasn't going to find the answers I was looking for with the shiny happy people. And I was still looking for answers. So I began reading books about Christianity and the origin of the Bible. I figured that if Christians got their beliefs from the Bible, the first question to investigate was where the Bible came from.

I also had this growing sense that I should find a church to help me in this search, a place where I could ask questions. There happened to be a church right across the street from my dorm, so once again, out of curiosity, I gave another Christian meeting a try. This time, my friend Randy came along with me to attend a Sunday service.

As soon as we walked into the church building, I knew that this was going to be very different from my experience with the shiny happy people. This was truly a church building — it had stained-glass windows, a pulpit, and a number of fancy religious symbols scattered around the room on colored banners. When we walked into the building, we heard organ music. I confess, just hearing an organ reminds me of a funeral parlor and puts me in a strange state of mind. I also noticed that the seating was all pews. Really the only place you see pews, outside of a church, is in a courtroom. So as we walked down the aisle with the organ music playing and found seats in the pews, I was thinking about two things: death and jury duty.

The people at this gathering were solemn and serious. Everyone kept their voices to a whisper. I found myself staring at the carpet. It was this orange-red color, and they must have recently had it cleaned, because it had a strong chemical odor. After staring at the carpet for several minutes, the combination of the color, the odor, the whispers, and the depressing sound of the organ left me feeling a bit light-headed.

And then it began.

The organ stopped, and a man walked out of a hidden side door (a special God-meeting room?) and stood on the stage. He was dressed in an elegant robe. I had seen religious leaders wearing robes on television before, so I wasn't too surprised by this, but I had never looked at one closely. It was a white robe with a green-and-gold-striped scarf draped over his shoulders. There were symbols on the scarf, but I didn't know what they meant. I think they were the "Chi-Ro" symbol, a Christian symbol formed by superimposing the first two letters in the Greek spelling of the word *Christ*. Not knowing this, I simply assumed they were the marks of some sort of secret society.

I remember thinking how strange it was seeing someone wearing a robe in the daytime. The only person I knew of who wore a robe during the day was Hugh Hefner. The arms of the robe grew wider near his hands, so whenever he spread out his arms, as he did for the greeting, it looked like he had wings, sort of like a superhero. I was into comic books, and the more I pondered it, the more I thought that the whole outfit had a subtle superhero costume look to it as well. Whenever he lifted his arms as he talked, I couldn't help imagining he was about to fly away with his superhero-logo-embossed scarf draped over his shoulder.

After welcoming us to the meeting, he had everyone read from a book kept on racks behind each pew. We were supposed to read sections from the book, alternating with his reading, in a deep monotone voice. It reminded me of the chanting I heard once in a horror movie in which these witches all sat around and chanted in a deep spooky voice together. Randy and I didn't really feel comfortable chanting with the others, so we watched everyone else reading. Then the organ played and some people sang a song or two, which I didn't recognize, while we just stood there staring at the pages of a songbook.

## THE INCREDIBLE, MAGICAL CUP OF WONDER

The man in the robe gave a talk of some sort, which felt more like a dramatic reading to me. He spoke with various inflections, and the words he used weren't ones we use in everyday language. He had a formal style of speaking. Then, without explanation, people began standing up and going down the aisle to the front, where they kneeled on a low bench that went across the front of the stage. You could tell they knew what they were doing; they went up row by row like they'd been doing this for years. The man in the robe held up a big golden goblet and said some words. At first I thought he was going to do some sort of magic trick and pull something out of the goblet. But then I realized it was a formal prayer he'd memorized. I wondered if he was praying to the goblet, since he was staring at it and speaking directly to it. After the prayer, he whispered something to the person kneeling on the far right of the stage and handed them the cup. I couldn't tell what happened after that, since everyone kneeling up front was blocking my view.

As each row went up one after the other, I soon realized that we would need to go up front with everyone else. If we stayed in our seats, we'd block the others in our row, since there wasn't room for people to pass us in the pew. We were stuck. I looked at Randy, and he had this panicked look on his face. But I was actually curious to find out what was happening up there, and so Randy followed me to the front, and we knelt on the padded step.

From this perspective, I could see the man in the robe again. He whispered to the person at the end of the row and handed him the golden cup. This person dipped a tiny little cracker in the cup, pulled it out, and ate it. Then he whispered something to the guy on his left and passed him the cup. This guy also dipped a tiny little cracker in and ate it, passing the cup to the person on his left and whispering something. The process repeated itself down the row until it was my turn. The woman next to me handed me the cup and said something about blood and "this is for you" and something about flesh. I did what I had seen the others do, not understanding what it meant or why I was doing it. When I finished, I realized that I was supposed to hand the cup off to Randy. The problem was, I couldn't make sense of what the lady had said to me when she passed me the cup. I knew I was supposed to repeat her words to Randy, but I couldn't remember any of them. So I just handed Randy the cup, shrugged, and didn't say anything.

Randy dipped his cracker in the cup. When he was done, he took the cup and held it out to the woman on his left, hesitating for a moment. He knew he was supposed to say *something* to the woman, but since I hadn't said anything to him, he was stumped. So he looked the person in the eye and with great confidence handed her the cup, saying, "Here is the Cup of Wonder."

I knew those were the wrong words, and when Randy said

"Cup of Wonder," the tension of the entire experience just overcame me and I burst out laughing. It was quite disruptive in the quietness and sober mood of what was happening around me. And to make it worse, I tried to stop laughing but couldn't, really, because it all happened so fast, and so it didn't sound like a real laugh. It sounded like some sort of muffled monkey shriek.

As I shrieked, Randy began giggling like a schoolgirl. We tried to avoid eye contact and stared downward to control ourselves, but it was pretty intense. My hands were clasped on the banister in front of me, and it was shaking as my body rocked from the effort to stop laughing. Everyone kneeling in the row looked over, and the man in the superhero robe stared at us with a questioning look. I really felt terrible about laughing, because this was such a horribly inappropriate time, but the more I tried to control it, the worse it got. I stood up and ran down the aisle, exiting out the back. I didn't look to see what Randy was doing, but he had the same idea and was right behind me. We laughed uncontrollably for half of our walk back to the dorm. We knew that what we had done was wrong, or at least highly inappropriate, and I felt bad about it, but it was such a strange experience for both of us, we really didn't know how to respond.

## LOOKING INTO THE CONFUSING AND STRANGE CHRISTIAN SUBCULTURE

As I think back on that experience, I try to imagine what I would do as a pastor if I was serving communion and two college students just burst out laughing in front of me and then ran out of the room. Communion is a holy and sacred time for remembering Jesus' death on the cross. The juice in the cup represents his blood, and the bread represents his body.[26] In many ways, the communion cup really is a cup of wonder. But it was unfortunate that we didn't understand any of this. I wish the man in the robe had simply explained what we were doing beforehand and let everyone know that they didn't have to receive communion if they didn't want to, especially if they didn't understand what was happening. If he had, we would have realized that it's okay to step out of the pew to let people pass and then sit down again, and the whole scene would have been avoided.

I should also add that over the years, I've come to better understand and respect the traditions of the church and can now see why certain church leaders might choose to wear robes or speak in a certain tone using certain words. But as a nineteen-year-old who didn't understand any of this, the organ music, the responsive readings, the robe, the whispers, and the cup all seemed very odd and confusing. It was like watching a man in a superhero outfit speak in a Shakespearian actor's voice and hold a magical cup in the air as people chanted spooky words in a deep monotone voice together. It was nothing at all like the peppy, clappy campus meeting I had visited earlier, which made it all the more confusing.

For the most part, my experiences with the shiny happy people and the whispering orange-carpet people were pretty harmless. But my encounters with them didn't lead me to get involved with these groups or to get to know any Christians, since they seemed so different from me or my friends. They probably were nice people, but I couldn't see myself going to their meetings. I soon discovered, however, that these weren't the only types of Christians out there. I learned that not all Christians just leave you alone, and not all of them are really happy. I was about to meet my first judgmental Christian. And he wasn't very shiny or nice.

# CHAPTER FOUR

# I SEE

★ ★ —— MEAN —— ★ ★

## PEOPLE

> I love the idea of the teachings of Jesus Christ and the beautiful stories.... But the reality is that organized religion doesn't seem to work. It turns people into hateful lemmings and it's not really compassionate.
>
> —*Elton John*

**"REPENT!** God's wrath is coming against you! Judgment is near!"

I could hear the words being shouted in the courtyard as I exited the Colorado State University library with a friend, so we followed the sound to see what was happening. We found a crowd of people gathered around a man who was standing on a planter shouting. He was about thirty years old, dressed in a suit and tie, but there he was, yelling and pointing at the crowd with a big Bible in his hand. I didn't even know what the word *repent* means. Most of the others probably didn't either. But he sure was yelling that word a lot.

I felt like I had stumbled into a cartoon. He was the perfect caricature of an angry street preacher, every stereotypical detail you can think of present in living color before my eyes. It was so over the top, as if someone had hired this guy to act the part and it all was just a joke. But no one was laughing when the preacher began pointing his finger at people in the crowd. He looked at people and called them sinners, and at one point, he pointed his finger at the girl who was with me and shouted "whore!" at her. It was quite shocking. He continued pointing out various individuals, calling them all sorts of names — "drunkards," "immoral people" — and accusing them of every sin you can think of. It wasn't very funny anymore.

I remember I was really bothered that this man was accusing people of some pretty horrible things, yet he had no idea who they were. He had never met the girl I was with or any of the other people in the crowd, but he was making serious accusations about their conduct and lifestyle. And all of that with a Bible in his hand. To the dozens of students walking by that day, he was representing what it means to be a follower of Jesus, a Christian. Based on my experiences, I knew that most Christians didn't stand on planters and call strangers whores, but I still felt horribly uncomfortable with the whole experience. You'd never see Buddhists or Hindus going around doing stuff like this.

Over the next few years that I attended the university, this same guy returned every couple of months. I later found out that he travelled to different campuses preaching his message. I still remember the last time I saw him. It was during the winter, and he was outside preaching the same message when a couple of guys ran up behind him while he was yelling and smashed a ton of snow over his head. He stopped what he was saying for a moment, and then went right back at it, preaching his message.

## CHRISTIAN POLLSTERS WHO WON'T LEAVE YOU ALONE

I started meeting other Christians on campus, people who walked up to me while I was studying or on my way to class. They usually asked me to take a survey, but the questions they asked were leading, confrontational questions, and I'd grow pretty uncomfortable trying to answer them. They weren't the kinds of questions people outside of Churchland normally brought up in a conversation with strangers. They asked if I thought there was more than one way to know God. Or they asked whether I believed in absolute truth. Or if I knew where I was going when I died. I started wondering why Christians were so consumed by the idea of death. I was only nineteen, and I wasn't planning on dying anytime soon, nor did I spend much time thinking about it. These Christian Pollsters reminded me of the Daniel Boone evangelist I met in junior high, only they were much more sophisticated and skilled in asking questions that made people uncomfortable.

What I found most irritating was that they frequently interrupted me when I was out minding my own business, not bothering anyone. It's a bit awkward to have to answer personal, life-and-death questions with someone you don't even know. When I turned the tables and asked them questions, their answers always sounded a bit rehearsed. I heard the same cliches again and again. It felt like they didn't really care about my answers or what I believed; they mostly were interested in filling out their little surveys and getting me to give the responses they wanted. Eventually, whenever I saw any of them coming, I left so I could avoid these awkward conversations.

I still had not given up on my search to understand whether Christianity is true. I began experimenting a bit with the radio, scanning for Christian stations that played sermons by various preachers. More often than not, the sermons seemed to eventually state how bad the world was getting and how we needed to protect ourselves from evil. Of course, by "evil" the radio preachers generally meant Hollywood, homosexuals, people of other religious faiths, those who believed differently than they did, and anyone or anything they felt was corrupting the world. I heard a lot of war rhetoric and talk about being in a spiritual battle. Listening to the radio, I got the impression that Christianity is mostly about avoiding certain things, criticizing other religions, and spending your days thinking about all the bad things that were happening in the world. Of course, almost every radio program encouraged me to send them money so they could stay on the air, and sometimes they'd offer to send a free book or a gift in return. I never understood how they could say that those things were free if you had to donate money to get them. I developed a mistrust of radio preachers.

## END TIMES MAPS, ANTICHRIST, AND CRUSADES

My experiences with evangelical Christianity were taking me from one extreme to the other. Either Christianity was about togetherness and peppiness and singing happy songs, or it was about crusading and going to battle against the evils of the world. Whenever I read about Christians putting on crusades in different cities or heard them talk about fighting a spiritual battle or using other war terminology, I was reminded of the Crusades of the Middle Ages. I wasn't sure how the happy friendly people I had met fit with the militant, battle-hungry side of Christianity.

I remember one time when I was staying at a girlfriend's father's house and I found a Christian book in the bedroom on the end of the world. I started reading it and ended up staying up the whole night to finish it. It was all about what the Bible says about the end times and the meaning of the book of Revelation, and it was pretty mind-blowing to me. The author had mapped out battles which were going to happen in Israel. There were maps with arrows showing what direction armies from various countries would invade, as well as charts that gave timelines for when Jesus was going to return to earth and join a massive battle against the evil nations.

I had never before heard that Jesus was coming back to earth. At that time, I was just learning about Jesus' life on earth, so this new information was quite a shocker. I had seen the movie *The Omen*, which had the Antichrist and 666 (the number of the beast) in it. But I didn't realize that Christians thought this stuff was real. I thought it was just fiction in the movies. It sounded so incredibly insane to me, but I wanted to read it all, and I confess that I stole the book from my girlfriend's dad's house. (And I still feel guilty about it.) But it was so incredible, I just had to learn more about all of this end-times stuff and what Christians believed. Did they all see Jesus as a general who would one day lead the armies of heaven into battle, destroying the armies of evil like this book described? I had never thought of Jesus that way before.

## THE INTERVENTION THAT WASN'T REALLY
## AN INTERVENTION

Very confused, I began purchasing more and more books on what Christians believe. I also became passionate about learning the origin of the Bible. I was really interested in learning why Christians think the Bible is a book from God. It seemed most religious faiths claimed their holy writings were from God, so why did Christians think that only theirs and not the others' was really from God? I also figured that since this is where all the talk about hell and judgment was coming from, it was worth learning the history of the book. I gave up attending any church meetings, but I started developing a little library of Christian books that I kept on the cinder-block and wood-plank shelves in my room. I became quite passionate about trying to understand what this thing called the Bible actually was. But it seemed like a complex book, and I had no idea how to read it. I couldn't make sense of the names of the books or why they were in that particular order. I spent most of my time just flipping through it, randomly stopping in different places, but as I did, I found find myself being drawn, more and more, to the New Testament books that described the birth, life, and death of Jesus. I really felt connected with Jesus' words and his teaching. There was a whole lot of Jesus' teaching that I didn't understand, but his words haunted me, and the way he cared for people was incredible. And I really enjoyed reading about the times when he challenged the hypocritical religious leaders of his day.

As my library of religious books grew, my friends and college roommates began asking me what I was doing. Why was I reading all of this stuff about Christianity? I remember one friend asked me straight out, "You're not going to become one of those Christians, are you?" Most of my friends were suspicious of the church and had many of the same impressions of Christians that I had, so you can understand why they were concerned when one of their friends became obsessively interested in the Bible.

One day I came home and a found a couple of my friends in the living room. When I walked in, it suddenly became uncomfortably quiet. I could tell that something was wrong. One of my friends spoke up: "Dan, we're wondering why you are reading all these books on Christianity. What's going on?" My other friend, out of deep concern for me, explained that Christians have no creativity and that they're all homogeneous because the church restricts their thinking and keeps everyone under their control out of a desire for uniformity. It felt almost like an unplanned intervention. Except that I wasn't addicted to drugs or struggling with alcohol. I was reading books about Christianity and the Bible.

Because these were my friends, I listened to their concerns and their warnings. I didn't talk about it with them afterward, but what they said deeply affected me. I understood why they were concerned about my becoming a Christian. Many of the things they said described my own experiences with Christians. It was a gut-wrenching experience for me, because deep inside I kept thinking, What if they are right? Could it be true? Will I lose my creativity if I become a Christian? Will I have to toss out rational thinking and take the whole Bible literally? Will I wind up clapping my hands and singing pep-rally songs with other Christians? Will I be hanging out with a man in a superhero robe who prays to a golden goblet in a whispery room of organ-music lovers? Or will I turn into a fearful finger-pointing person or a warmongering Christian eagerly awaiting Jesus' return to earth to launch battles in the Middle East? I was pretty confused, to say the least. I knew that I didn't want to become one of those Christians.

But were there other options?

From what I was reading in the Bible, Jesus didn't fit the stereotypes I had of his followers. The more I read the Bible, the more I was drawn to Jesus. Slowly he was becoming a part of my life. His words and his example began to influence my thinking, and I just couldn't shake him out of my head. I knew that something was happening inside of me, but without other examples of what it means to be a Christian, this tension in my life was wearing me down, mentally and emotionally.

If things kept going the same way, I likely would have given up on Jesus and the church. But something happened that changed my thinking about Christianity.

It wasn't that I read a book or heard a charismatic speaker or went to a big Christian concert.

What happened was I met an elderly man in England who liked drinking Ovaltine.

# CHAPTER FIVE

# OVALTINE, THE BIBLE, AND ELDERLY LADIES FIGHTING IN THE BASEMENT

**HE WAS AN EIGHTY-THREE-YEAR-OLD** quintessential English gentleman. He couldn't name a single contemporary musical band. He hadn't seen any of the latest movies. He didn't know what television shows were popular, nor did he know the names of any up-and-coming celebrities in pop culture. He lacked all knowledge of things hip, cool, and culturally relevant. He wasn't a finger-pointing, right-wing, dogmatic, anti-intellectual fundamentalist, nor was he one of the homogenous, singing, shiny, happy Christians. He was just an elderly man who studied the Bible and tried to follow Jesus in the best and most authentic way he knew.

I met Stuart Allen while I was living in London, England, after graduating from Colorado State University. I was in a punk-rockabilly band with my brother, Tommy, who played guitar, and my friend Mark Frauenfelder, who played bass.[27] Several of the bands that we loved and the people who influenced us musically were from London, so we decided to move there after college to have

*Courtesy of Nestlé*

a go at it as a band. We didn't have a plan. It was more of a music adventure, really. We had no idea where we would live when we arrived, but that's what made it such a wonderfully rich experience, never really knowing what would happen next. I just stuffed my silver-sparkle Ludwig drum set in a large television box and made my way to England.

## FORGET CHURCH, I'LL STICK WITH JESUS AND THE BIBLE

While we were living in London, I made a personal commitment to read the Bible from cover to cover. Since most of my reading had been flipping around to various sections of the Bible, I thought I should try working my way through the entire thing, front to back. I bought a tiny brown Bible from a bookstore in London. It was small enough to fit in my jacket or the back pocket of my jeans, and I took it with me everywhere I went. Every time our band played somewhere, I took a gym bag containing my drumsticks, a towel, my hair gel, a couple of cans of beer, and my little brown Bible. I'd read the Bible while riding on the train or the bus around London. Whenever I had a spare moment, I'd slip in some reading. I kept that little Bible next to my bed every night and often fell asleep with it next to my head, sometimes even using it as a pillow.

I worked all sorts of temporary jobs in London: stocking books at a large bookstore on Charing Cross Road; doing dishes in the steamy cafeteria kitchen of an office building, after which I'd come home smelling like dishwashing soap. One of my temp jobs was working in the famous Parliament building. In Parliament, I worked in the basement and was on call throughout the day. Whenever I was called, I brought up a dozen gallons of milk or twenty loaves of bread or whatever was needed in the kitchen to prep meals. Sometimes I actually got to set up tea and cookies for Parliament members. It was quite an odd experience. I would be pushing my little cart of snacks through the halls of this historical building, wearing my Converse sneakers and my Clash T-shirt under my green apron, with government leaders walking all around me.

And, of course, I had my tiny brown Bible in my pocket.

Wherever I was working, I developed a pattern of going off to a nearby pub or sitting in a park and using my lunch breaks to read and study the Bible. I was having a hard time understanding most of the strange stories, and some of the violence I read about was confusing to me. I'd take out a little red pencil and make a dot on the page next to Bible verses that I had questions about. That little brown Bible developed a lot of red marks. I marked some of the parts that sounded crazy to me, like when John the Baptist was eating insects, or how God seemed to approve of killing entire groups of people in the Old Testament. I marked some of the strange sayings of Jesus that I just could not figure out and several of those end-times passages with horrific scenes of destruction and death. I really didn't know what to think of some of the unusual things I was reading.

And the number of red dots in my little brown Bible grew.

## HOW OVALTINE CHANGED MY LIFE

One of my temporary jobs was at an insurance agency in the London banking district. Working in a room all by myself, I hand-stuffed hundreds and hundreds of envelopes for their mailers.

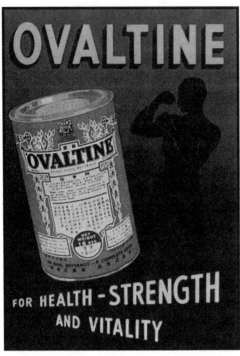

Courtesy of Nestlé

It was incredibly tedious. I always looked forward to my lunch breaks, when I could leave the office and go to a nearby bowling green to watch the lawn bowlers, eat lunch, and read my Bible. (If you've never seen lawn bowling before, it's quite fascinating.)

Each day, while walking to the bowling green, I passed a tiny little brick church building crammed between two large office buildings. It was such a small place, and it was normally closed, so I didn't pay much attention to it. But one day there was a fairly beaten up sandwich board sign on the sidewalk with a message scrawled on white paper: "Bible Study Today at Noon — All Welcome!"

I stood there for a moment and checked my watch. It was just past noon. I had my Bible in my pocket. Why not? I was curious, so I cautiously cracked open one of the old wooden doors and craned my neck around it to look inside. The light from outside shone into a darkened room, and I saw an elderly man sitting with another older man and woman. They looked up at me with surprised expressions on their faces. I had the feeling that they had been sitting in this room for twenty years, just waiting for someone to read the sign on the street and come in. And now, I had come, and they were a bit shocked to actually see someone.

They had a small circle of chairs set up right by the entryway. As I peeked in the door, the leader said warmly in a English accent, "Hello! Here for the study?"

My instinct was to say, "Oops! Wrong building!" and back out and let the door close. It was such a tiny group. The room was a bit dark, in a spooky sort of way. And they were three elderly people.

But the leader spoke with such kindness in his eyes and evident joy that someone actually might be joining them, I felt bad for them, so I sheepishly said yes. The leader smiled and waved me over to the chair next to him.

I sat down, and without even asking me, the leader of the study began pouring something from his thermos into a glass. He handed it to me. "Here's some Ovaltine!"

I didn't know what to think. Ovaltine? Oh my, Christians are so incredibly weird. They're into Ovaltine? I hadn't had Ovaltine since I was a child. I was expecting him to offer me tea or coffee, never thinking I'd be getting chocolate Ovaltine. Still, I took the glass and said thank you. I was so nervous that I drank the whole thing down in just a few quick gulps. The leader, who turned out to be Stuart Allen, watched me intently as I drank, and he seemed pretty pleased when I drank it down so enthusiastically. He smiled in approval as I handed the glass back to him, and he poured me a second glass. "Have some more!" As I drank the next glass, he turned to the other elderly people with this satisfied look of "it's working."

I then had this fleeting sense of panic that I had just swallowed chemically laced Ovaltine and would later wake up chained in a dungeon with a cult of strange elderly people poking me with metal prods or preparing me for some secret ancient Druid ritual. My fear was unfounded. It turned out they were just a handful of elderly followers of Jesus who liked to share a favorite drink of theirs with a stranger off the street. It just so happened that their favorite drink was Ovaltine.

I sat in that Bible study with the three elderly people for my entire lunch hour that day. I'm not exaggerating when I say that it was a meeting that changed my life. Or perhaps I should say that it was a meeting that *began* to change my life by reshaping how I understood the relationship between Christians and the Bible. The group spent most of the time talking about the Bible, and as they looked up various passages, they talked about the cultural context of each letter or book: when it was written, to whom it was written, and why it was written. They weren't just reading the Bible to find three application points for their lives. They took the time to understand the ancient culture of the Bible and how that should make a difference in their reading and interpretation of the Bible. They even had a map they pulled out occasionally to get a better picture of the different cities and places they read about. I had never experienced this way of studying the Bible before, and it was so much more meaningful than any of my own previous attempts.

## IT'S NOT BAD TO ASK QUESTIONS ABOUT THE BIBLE

I had so many questions about everything they discussed, and was amazed to discover that they didn't mind when I asked them. Since they encouraged me to ask questions, I started asking them to explain some of the verses in my Bible that had red dots next to them. Not once did they ever make me feel silly for asking a question or demean me for my lack of biblical knowledge. I soon learned that one of their favorite verses (which ended up becoming a favorite of mine as well) is from a passage in the New Testament that talks about a city called Berea, which was located in what is today part of Greece. This verse says that "the Bereans were of more noble character than the Thessalonians [another city in Greece], for they received the message with great eagerness and examined the Scriptures every day to see if what Paul said was true."[28] The Bereans were commended for asking questions and checking out what someone taught. In my previous interactions with Christians, I had never gotten the impression that asking questions was a good thing, much less a sign of noble character. Most of the Christians I encountered seemed to have an attitude that said, "What we say is true, take it or leave it, and certainly don't question it." So it was wonderfully refreshing to have a Christian tell me that it's a good thing to ask questions! It also put me at ease a bit, knowing that there was no brainwashing program in place to destroy my intelligence.

Spending time with these people helped me to understand that there are some Christians who don't just read the Bible at a shallow level and then jump to conclusions.

## OVALTINE MADE ME HAPPY

I returned to that Wednesday noon Bible study the next week. And I even began meeting with Stuart every Tuesday for lunch. I learned that he was an intelligent man who had attended Oxford

University and studied classical music and ancient languages. He would ride the train for almost an hour to get to London to meet with me. He always brought his thermos of Ovaltine, and I began to enjoy having a cup to drink with him every week. I asked Stuart all of my questions, from the lake of fire and the Antichrist to all of the strange things I had been reading about. Stuart was able to answer my questions by explaining what these things might have meant to people living at the time when the Bible was written. He explained to me how the writers used imagery and symbolism. He told me that there is such a thing as judgment and there is even a place called hell, but he also explained how various metaphors and descriptions were used to communicate these realities. He avoided the sensationalism I had found in some of the books I had read and the sermons I had heard on the radio.

Whenever Stuart didn't know the answer to a question, or if there was more than one way to understand a verse, he simply told me that there will always be things we just won't know with certainty in this life. He often taught me that while God knows what he meant to communicate to us, we don't always fully grasp the meaning or intention of a passage. This wasn't meant to be a cop-out or an excuse to give up; it was a statement born of humble study. Stuart helped me to see that there are some mysteries in the Bible that are just really hard to figure out.

I eventually started going to the Sunday church meetings as well and found that the church was made up of about fifteen to twenty people, almost all of them over the age of sixty. I discovered that Stuart was also the organist for the church, and he led the singing on Sunday mornings. He would lead us in a few hymns, get up from the organ, and then very gradually make his way to the pulpit. Because of his age, Stuart took very small baby steps, and I always found it a bit amusing, that gap of total silence as he walked ever so slowly to the front to begin his sermon.

These little church services had zero focus on production. There was no flash, no charismatic speaker, and no pop worship band. It was just an eighty-three-year-old man doing his best to play the organ and preach a sermon. His voice wasn't all that strong, and I often had to strain to hear him and follow what he was saying. But in this tiny church, my heart started changing, and for the first time I began to think that maybe, just maybe, being a Christian wasn't all that bad. I was starting to see that not every Christian fit the stereotypes I had come to believe.

## ELDERLY, LOVING, NONJUDGMENTAL, JESUS-LOVING THEOLOGIANS

What's a bit strange about all of this is that at the very same time, I was totally immersed in the London music scene. I was fully into vintage, punk, and rockabilly fashion and hairstyle. Often, I would be out very late Saturday night hanging with the band (and doing everything that goes along with being in a band), and I'd stumble into the service on Sunday mornings looking as if I'd been out all night, which often was true. But not once did any of the people in that church make a negative comment about the way I dressed or wore my hair in a pompadour. They never asked why I was in a punk-rockabilly band or criticized me for hanging out in the pubs until the wee hours of the night. Even after I had attended for several months and they had grown to know me a bit, they never once remarked about my appearance or behavior in a negative way.

They did, however, share with me how beautiful it is that God created all different kinds of music. Stuart, in particular, was quite passionate about art and music. Far from discouraging creativity, Stuart talked about the truth that God is creative and about how we reflect that creativity, since we are made in his image. We often talked about the history of art and the history of different musical genres. He took me to the Royal Albert Hall to hear Handel's *Messiah* performed and encouraged my exposure to different genres of music. Instead of stifling my creativity, Stuart, who was a pastor, actually encouraged it and helped me to develop it.

## ELDERLY LADIES FIGHTING IN A MUSTY OLD CHURCH BASEMENT

For the next several months, this tiny group of elderly Londoners adopted me as a grandson. After the Sunday worship meetings, we all went down into the musty old basement to have lunch together. I didn't have to bring my lunch because the wonderful white-haired ladies always brought me sandwiches and cookies. When I sat down at the table, they slid several plates in front of me. It even got a little feisty sometimes when they argued over whose sandwich I would be eating that day. It was great because almost every week, I went home from church with a brown paper bag filled with several extra sandwiches they had brought for me.

This musty basement is where I first came to experience real Christian community. It was a place where I was able to ask questions without being ridiculed or challenged for asking them. It was a place where I was loved and accepted, even though I was very different from them, a place where people didn't try to change my appearance or make me conform to their music or lifestyle, but rather cared deeply about my heart and wanted me to better understand Jesus.

It was a beautiful and rather eccentric mix: a young Guinness-drinking, punk-rockabilly musician from northern New Jersey spending his Sunday mornings with a group of quaint, elderly, tea-sipping, scholarly English saints in the musty basement of a small church building in the banking district of London. But Jesus was our common bond, and I am convinced that only God could have brought us together.

## "GOD'S KINDNESS IS INTENDED TO LEAD YOU TO REPENTANCE" —ROMANS 2:4

During the time I was exploring Christianity at that little church in London, if someone had focused on judging my behavior or attempting to change my lifestyle or my appearance, I probably never would have remained. Thankfully, these people simply showed me the kindness of God, loving me and accepting me just as I was, eager to answer my questions. They cared about my getting to know Jesus, not about my conforming to the Christian subculture.

God's kindness to me through this small London church gave me the desire to change in the areas of my life that weren't in alignment with the Scriptures.

Perhaps if we, as followers of Jesus, were seen more as instruments of God's kindness to people than as oracles of judgment and pointing out wrongs, people would want to know the God we claim to represent.

## THE LOUDEST VOICES SHAPE OUR PERSPECTIVE

I sometimes wonder what my life would have been like if I hadn't met Stuart and the wonderful people in that tiny old church. I probably would have continued to think of Christians in stereotyped categories based on my negative experiences, such as with the shiny, happy people or with aggressive Christians who stand in public places holding up cartoonlike signs about judgment and hell. And I would have continued to arrive at my conclusions about Christianity based more on the extreme examples I experienced who don't represent the entire church. Sadly, it's the loudest voices (and the biggest signs) that often shape the way many people see Christians and the church.

I do understand that there are stories of people who have been disillusioned by the church. Some experienced hypocrisy or were not in a church that was a safe place to ask questions. Some encountered Christians who lacked grace toward those they didn't agree with on political or social issues. But please know that when Jesus started his church, he meant it to be something beautiful, and I believe that it is still very possible for his church to be beautiful today.

# CHAPTER SIX

# CANNIBALS
## ★ ★ —AND— ★ ★
# CREEPY PASTORS

> You Christians are the worst breed ever to affect the world. You deserve every punishment you can get! Nobody likes you. It would be better if you and your Jesus had never been born. We hear that you are all cannibals — you eat the flesh of your children in your sacred meetings.
>
> —Caecilius (Rome, AD 230)

**I CONFESS** that I don't go to the gym very often. I do believe that God wants us to take care of our bodies and live a healthy lifestyle, and I'd love to establish some kind of routine, but I'm not an athlete (unless you count bowling and shooting pool), so I still get all intimidated whenever I go to the gym. When I walk into a gym, it seems that everyone there naturally and gracefully uses the equipment. I, on the other hand, am very uncomfortable. The workout room is surrounded by mirrors, and as I watch myself working out, it looks so incredibly unnatural, making the experience all the more awkward for me.

Even the gym fashions intimidate me. I sheepishly walk into the gym with my black Converse sneakers, my Ramones T-shirt, and the sweatpants that I wore as pajamas the night before. I look around the room and see people wearing coordinated outfits. Somehow, they seem to know exactly what kind of sweats to wear and what shoes look right with them. Even the gruff muscle guys seem to have fashionable gym outfits, making my insecurities even more pronounced.

Still, despite my discomfort, I try to get to the gym as often as I can, since I believe that it's important that we care for our bodies.[29]

## "PASTORS ARE CREEPY!"

One time, after a prolonged absence from the gym, I returned and discovered that they had some new equipment. A woman in her early twenties who worked at the gym agreed to show me how to use it. As we worked our way through the different machines, we carried on a conversation, which quickly turned to the topic of music. Since music is one of my passions, I find that I am able to involve myself in discussions about bands and musical styles, even with people I've just met. We talked about some of the bands we both enjoyed: The Smiths, Morrissey, and The Cure.

After she finished showing me how to use all of the machines, I thanked her for her help, and she asked me what I did for a living. As soon as I mentioned that I was a pastor, she pulled away from me. She actually took several steps backward, as if she were afraid of catching a virus or disease, and bumped into the workout machine behind her.

She looked at me with an expression of disbelief and said, "No, you're not!"

I assured her that I was, indeed, a pastor.

Again, she objected, and we went back and forth a few times. I could tell that we weren't getting anywhere, so I asked her why she didn't believe me. Without blinking, she blurted, "Pastors are creepy!"

Pastors are creepy? That wasn't what I was expecting to hear. So I asked her to explain.

She talked about the pastors she had seen on CNN, how they are often arguing and cutting each other down with "pinched angry faces." She talked about the hypocrisy of church leaders and the frequent news reports about pastors speaking out against something and then getting caught doing the very thing they were speaking against. And she brought up the money and sex scandals that appear in the news from time to time. She talked about seeing pastors interviewed on television, always protesting something, and about seeing flamboyant television evangelists asking for money in exchange for God's blessing. The more I listened to her, the more I agreed — some pastors *are* creepy.

I asked, "Do you know any pastors personally?"

She thought about it. "No. I've never actually met any. Just you."

I'm not suggesting that her observations about creepy pastors are wrong. Most of them are probably true, and I agree that there are some creepy pastors out there — and some creepy Christians and creepy churches too. And since the only pastors this girl had ever seen were the people on television, her dislike of pastors made perfect sense. But in my experience, working in the church and interacting with church leaders, the overwhelming majority of pastors aren't anything like the people she had seen on television. And I truly believe that most Christians and churches aren't creepy either.

## CHRISTIANS ARE CANNIBALISTIC, INCESTUOUS ATHEISTS

Interestingly, from the very beginning of the church, there has always been confusion about Christians. In various cultures and at different times throughout history, the church has been both loved and hated, reviled and applauded. When we study early church history, we learn that the early Christians and the leaders of the church were often misunderstood. In the first few centuries, as Christianity spread throughout the Roman Empire, outsiders to the faith had several misperceptions and made some strong accusations about Christians.

> *Christians practice cannibalism.* When the early followers of
> Jesus gathered, they followed Jesus' teachings by sharing
> a meal, often called communion or the Lord's Supper,
> which commemorated Jesus' death.[30] The wine or grape
> juice symbolized the blood Jesus shed when he died on
> the cross, and the bread symbolized his body. But the

symbolic nature of the meal was misunderstood by people outside of the church. Rumors spread that the early Christians "drank blood and ate flesh," and they were accused of being cannibals.

*Christians have incestuous marriages.* Based on Jesus' teaching that God is the Father and that Jesus' followers are God's "adopted" sons and daughters, early Christians commonly called each other "brother" or "sister."[31] Outsiders assumed that married Christians who called each other brother and sister were both biologically related and married. To them, it appeared that Christians practiced incest.

*The Christian church is filled with atheists.* In the first century, the Christian church quickly spread throughout the Roman world. In Greco-Roman society, gods and goddesses typically were represented by statues displayed at the temple or some other place of worship. Because the early Christians did not create statues to represent the God they worshiped, they were thought to be atheists, people who rejected the worship of any god at all.

*Christians practice sorcery and magic.* Because the rituals of the Lord's Supper and baptism were new and different, Christians were accused of dabbling in spells and magical incantations. Some were thought to practice "mischievous superstition," and many believed that their minds were perverted. Christians were thought to practice "sorcery, with rites, spells, and magical formulas, amulets, and artifacts."[32]

## CLEARING UP THE CONFUSION

In the second century, a man named Marcus Minucius Felix wrote a letter to a fellow Roman named Caecilius, addressing some of the common accusations against Christians. Caecilius had been a vocal critic of Christianity, believing they were cannibals, strange people who didn't fit in with Roman society. In response, Marcus Felix shared with Caecilius his own process of learning about the Christian faith and how he had gained an accurate understanding of it: "For we were once the same as you; blind and ignorant, our opinions were once the same as yours. We believed that the Christians worshiped monsters, ate the flesh of infants, and practiced incest at their feasts. We did not understand that these tales were always being spread ... without examination or proof."[33]

Marcus Felix understood that many of the accusations about Christians were wrong, based on misinformation and misunderstandings. And though he himself was not a Christian, he felt compelled to speak up, to clear up the confusion. While today you aren't likely to hear accusations of cannibalism, atheism, incest, or sorcery directed at the Christian church, there are other confusing perceptions people have of Christians in our culture.

As we should do with anything we form opinions about, it's important that we base our understanding of the church on accurate information. People have perceptions about today's church based on generalizations or the extreme voices. Many believe that all Christians today are judgmental and homophobic, that all Christians oppress women, and arrogantly believe they are right and every other religion is wrong. Some people believe that all Christians are biblical literalists, fundamentalists who are afraid to ask tough questions and wrestle with difficult problems. Others dismiss the Christian church as nothing more than an organized religion only interested in acquiring and preserving power.

Let me assure you that there is truth to some of these observations and experiences. But even so, they don't accurately represent the whole church and the Christian faith. These negative experiences reflect a minority of Christians. The problem is that the loudest voices are the ones that end up defining Christianity and representing the church to the world.

The good news is that there are responses to the confusing and often negative perceptions of the church and Christianity. The church also has learned from some past mistakes, and there is a lot of change happening. I understand that not all Christians and churches will change. Some will hold on to ways of thinking and acting that can be destructive and negative. But there is this uprising of so many Christians and churches who are speaking out, challenging the church and calling it to faithfully follow Jesus.[34] There are many Christians who want to stop letting a small percentage of Christians define Christianity for everyone else.

## "YOU HAVE HEARD ... BUT I TELL YOU ..."

Early in my adventures in Churchland, I learned that redefining incorrect understandings was something that Jesus himself taught his followers to do. Jesus frequently challenged the religious systems of his day, questioning long-held assumptions and toppling sacred cows. The religious leaders at that time tried to paint their own picture of what it meant to be a worshiper of God, but Jesus regularly corrected them.

In the book of Matthew in the New Testament, Jesus has an interesting way of clarifying God's expectations for his people. Multiple times, as he teaches the people, he contrasts what he is telling them with the things they have heard and accepted. He says to them, "You have heard ... but I tell you ..."[35] Jesus wasn't interested in maintaining the status quo. He was interested in maintaining the truth. And in his teaching, he regularly tried to fix faulty understandings about God.

Jesus' approach should encourage us not to just blindly accept what we're told, that it's okay to ask questions, particularly if they challenge long-held assumptions. To be clear, I'm not arguing that any one of us can speak with the same authority as Jesus. But for those who are exploring the Christian faith, Jesus' example shows that he cared enough about the truth to confront the religious establishment. Jesus wasn't content to let misunderstandings about God and his people persist. He actually encouraged people to ask questions, to rethink some of their long-held beliefs and practices.

If Jesus were out preaching today, how might he respond to misperceptions about the church that he founded? How might he respond to criticisms leveled against his church? I believe that if he were speaking today, Jesus probably would try to clear up our misunderstandings in the same way he cleared up misunderstandings of God's expectations two thousand years ago. Perhaps he'd say something like this:

Obviously, I don't know exactly how Jesus would respond to today's criticisms of the church, but we do have the accounts of his life and his teachings and some of the letters written by his earliest followers. These were recorded in the Bible for us to read and study today. Frequently, the Bible talks about what the church — the community of Jesus' followers — should be doing, what it should look like, and why it even exists. Jesus may not be physically present to respond to our questions, but we still have an excellent way of understanding his intentions for his followers by looking into the Bible.

## UNCOMFORTABLE QUESTIONS ABOUT CHRISTIANS AND THE CHURCH

I could address so many questions in a book like this,[36] but I find that two issues come up over and over when I talk with people. The first is the perceived judgmentalism of Christians. Many people who are attracted to Jesus have been turned off by encounters with Christians who come across as self-righteous and condemning. The second issue is that many people dislike any form of organized or institutional religion. Many people believe that attempts to organize spiritual expression degrade it into man-made structures for asserting power and control, and many have had bad experiences with this.

Understandably, from outside the church, these two issues look like compelling reasons to dismiss the church and the Christian faith. But when we look under the surface — when we explore more deeply what the Bible teaches about the church — we do find answers. In part 2 of this book, we'll look closely at these two issues.

PART TWO

# FINDING BEAUTY

★ ★     ★ ★

# IN THE MESS

# CHAPTER SEVEN

# YOU HAVE HEARD
## —IT SAID...—
# THE CHURCH
★ ★ —IS— ★ ★
# JUDGMENTAL
—AND—
# NEGATIVE

Do not judge, or you too will be judged.

—*Jesus (Matthew 7:1)*

**AFTER A WONDERFUL YEAR** in England, I moved back to the United States and ended up living in California. The bass player in our band got a job in San Jose, and my girlfriend at the time was attending a university in that area as well, so we all moved to Northern California. I had absolutely no idea how to find a church, but I knew that I needed to be part of one. After my wonderful experience with Stuart Allen and the church in London, I couldn't imagine not being part of a church community. Even though I was still sorting through a lot of questions, after experiencing the beauty of the church, I knew I needed to find another church community when I moved back to America.

Still, I had no idea how to go about it, so I turned to the phone book. (This was before Google.) I'll share a bit about that confusing experience later, but eventually I did find a church community and began the next stage of my adventure in Churchland.

## DRUMMING LOVE BALLADS TO JESUS

The new church I began attending was quite large, filled with people of all different ages, which was a big shift for me after my experience in London. The church I had attended in England sang older hymns accompanied by an organ, but this new church sang contemporary Christian worship music with a band, and I read in the church bulletin that they needed a drummer. I thought playing drums for the worship band would give me an easy way to get involved, so I volunteered.

If you aren't familiar with worship music in contemporary evangelical churches, it's important to know that it's very different from the music traditional churches use. The songs we sang on Sunday mornings reminded me of the songs I heard the shiny, happy Christians singing in college. Some of the songs were similar to commercial jingles — upbeat, peppy, and repetitive — but the lyrics were about Jesus. In addition to the jingles we sang, there were several songs reminiscent of love ballads, except that instead of singing about a boyfriend or girlfriend, we sang about Jesus. I had never thought of singing love ballads to Jesus, to be perfectly honest. But the people at this church seemed to love them.

At first, I really struggled playing the drums for these songs. They were so incredibly different from the punk and rockabilly music I was used to playing. Drumming for the choir also required a mental shift. I was used to sitting down to play in a pub or club with a pint of Guinness on the floor next to me, but obviously I couldn't do that when I played for the choir. Also, the mood in church was entirely different from the mood in many of the places

I had played in. While in college, our band frequently played at fraternity parties, and it seemed like anything could happen. Two different times while I was drumming during rush week, when new fraternity members were being recruited, a naked male college student was tied up and dropped on the floor in front of me as part of his initiation rite. That didn't happen in church. Now, when I looked out from where I was drumming, instead of frat party dancing and drinking in dark clubs, I saw a mass of people singing songs of worship to God.

I developed a good friendship with one of the pastors who led the worship ministry. I got involved in a Bible study group with some other people my age, and this pastor and I used to meet to go over the study together. After a while, he asked me if I would be willing to help out with the youth group. At first, I was overwhelmed and humbled that anyone would even think of asking me to help. After all, I had never set foot in a church youth meeting before. But I remember almost crying when he asked me. I felt totally inadequate, but I was so honored that he believed in me enough to ask.

So I said yes.

I remember praying and thanking God over and over that I had been asked to do this. Could God really use me to help the youth in this church? I had never imagined that I might be asked to be a leader in a church. I was just a drummer in a band. Because of my background, I wasn't sure that I could be much of a role model for teenagers in a church context. But I was determined not to let this pastor down, though I was quite nervous and uncertain.

I was just starting to feel good about everything, eager to learn and to do whatever I could to help teach and lead the teenagers of this church. Then, in the midst of all my excitement, something happened that threw me for quite a loop.

I got judged.

## THE HORRIBLE FEELING OF BEING JUDGED

That Sunday, they announced to the church that I would be helping to lead the youth ministry. After the service, one of the other pastors pulled me aside. He said that he was glad I was willing to help out, and that he wanted to meet with me to give me some tips about working with the youth. I was thrilled! We arranged to get together at his office. Since I looked up to the pastors in the church, I felt honored even more that one of them asked to meet with me.

The church offices were a little strange. They all had identical furniture, and every office had the same large mahogany desk. They all had the same layout, with the desk facing the door. Behind the desks were some tall bookcases filled with books. When meeting with a pastor in his office, you sat with a momma-sized desk between you and him, facing a vast wall of books behind him. The entire setup was a bit intimidating, though I don't think that was intentional. Still, it communicated a clear distinction between the pastor and the person meeting with him.

On the afternoon of our meeting, the pastor greeted me warmly. I took a seat in front of his desk, and he walked over to the door and shut it. He made a comment about how happy he was that I was helping out with the youth. Then, he sat down, smiled, and began the conversation.

"Okay, there are some things you'll need to do if you're going to work with youth here. First, you really need to get a haircut."

I sat there stunned, not knowing what to say. This was not what I was expecting. Not in the least. I was thinking that we might talk about the dynamics of teaching teenagers the Bible, or that he'd pass along some leadership skills I needed to learn.

So I sat there and didn't say a word.

He smiled again, pulled a twenty dollar bill out of his wallet, and said, "Here. This haircut is on me." With a sweeping motion of his arm, he slid the bill across that wide desk and it stopped right in front of me, like a hockey puck reaching its goal.

Again, I didn't know what to say. This was the very last thing I had expected.

My hair at the time was pretty much like it is today. It's something of a pompadour cut, a haircut that is short on the sides and back but stands a lot higher on top than your typical men's haircut. I had styled it that way since my college years because it was a hairstyle that was popular among people in the '50s music scene that I liked, people like Elvis Presley, Little Richard, and Johnny Cash. Many of my music heroes from rockabilly and punk bands also wore their hair high in some form of a pompadour. It was simply a creative expression associated with the music genres I liked. I had never thought that I'd be asked to cut my hair to serve in a ministry of the church. These two things seemed completely unrelated to me.

So I sat there as the pastor explained to me how my haircut was not a normal haircut, and that church leaders needed to be careful about these types of things. He told me that my haircut could give the wrong impression to the youth or to the people attending the church. Then he said what really hurt me the most. He let me know that he'd *already* heard from some parents in the church who, after learning that I'd be working with the youth, were concerned about my appearance. Apparently, they felt that my hair and clothing weren't appropriate for a Christian leader.

As he was saying all of this, it was as if everything in my body, mind, and soul was aching. I felt horribly embarrassed, wondering how many others in the church also felt this way about my appearance. I was already sensitive to the fact that my background as a punk and rockabilly musician might be seen as a negative. Being a fairly new Christian, I was devastated. I assumed that because the church and this pastor felt this way about my hairstyle, God probably felt that way too. I felt foolish, ashamed that my hair could be displeasing to God, since I badly wanted to be doing what God wanted me to do.

Then the pastor pointed down at my shoes. I was wearing Doc Martins, and they had bright yellow stitching between the sole and the leather of the shoe.

"You may want to take a black Sharpie and color those stitches black. They are pretty flamboyant."

Flamboyant?

I had never paid attention to the color of the stitches on my shoes before. But again, I figured I should trust this pastor's opinion, and if that was what I needed to do to help out with the youth, then I guessed that was what I was supposed to do.

I felt embarrassed and judged and pretty terrible at that moment. I hadn't realized that my haircut and shoes were that important. My heart felt right. My motives seemed pure. But apparently several of the Christians in this church judged me because of my appearance, ignoring my heart and my faith and my desire to work with the youth.

Then the pastor said, "I'd like to help with your clothing too. You need to change how you dress, because people expect leaders to dress appropriately."

Back then, I usually wore vintage clothing, such as shirts from the '50s. (I still do.) Shopping for vintage clothing was something fun I'd do with my friends. Now I was learning that vintage clothing was not appropriate for people who worked with the youth.

The pastor, wanting to be helpful, offered me some new clothes. "I have some clothes I can give you for Sundays. Why don't you come over to our house, and I'll give you some tips on how to dress."

I left his office that day with my head down and my heart crushed. I took his twenty dollars to the barber. Off came the hair. I remember sitting in that barber's chair, watching my pompadour being cut off, thinking about Stuart Allen.

Stuart never told me that I would have to get a haircut.

He never said anything about the clothing I wore.

But then again, I had never served with youth at the church in London (they didn't have any, after all), so perhaps that was why they never asked me to change.

A few days later, I went to the pastor's house and received some tips for dressing on Sundays. He showed me several of his button-up shirts, golf shirts, slacks, and even a few suits and ties. I tried some on, and he showed me how to match colors.

As I was trying on all of these clothes, looking at myself in the mirror in disbelief, I thought, Oh God, is this really how you want me to dress? God, is this really what you want me to do?

## PUFFY GRAY KHAKIS MAKE NOT THE PERSON WHO LOVES JESUS

I remember one pair of gray khaki slacks in particular. They had really big pleats in the front — not your normal pleats but ones that puffed out a couple of inches. They looked quite odd. I was horrified to see myself in them in the mirror. What made it even worse was that when I walked out to show them to the pastor, his entire face just lit up, and he said, "You look great in those! Those would be great for when you teach the youth on Sunday."

My heart just sank.

But again, I was willing to do whatever it took to serve the youth at the church. So I nodded, gave a halfhearted smile, and uttered an okay and a thank-you.

So there I was, shifting into this new wardrobe and trying my best to fit into the world of Churchland, yet I still had this tension in my gut. I wasn't sure what any of this had to do with serving the youth. Is this what serving in the church is really all about? Do Christians really decide if you are acceptable based on what you wear and how you style your hair? Oh dear God, do I really have to wear these puffy pants? I had never worn khakis before. And now, oh my goodness, I was wearing the poofiest ones I'd ever seen. As I looked at myself in the mirror, I felt like I was slipping on a costume to act in a play or putting on a uniform of some sort.

Now, please know that this pastor was a genuinely caring person. I believe he did all of this with the very best of intentions. He wasn't trying to be mean or hurtful; he was doing his best to help me be successful in the youth ministry. And he was only trying to coach me, showing me how he thought a youth leader should dress and look around the students and parents on Sundays.

I almost didn't include this story in the book, because this pastor was quite sincere. But I share it because it was the first time I realized that in Churchland, some Christians' expectations are based not on the Bible but on personal preferences. There is not a single verse in the Bible that says how a youth worker should dress or style their hair. These concerns had nothing to do with Jesus' teachings. They were people's opinions about how *they* thought someone teaching their kids should look. Because I didn't meet their expectations, I was judged. And it felt terrible.

## GOODBYE TO THE PUFFY PANTS

I left the pastor's house that afternoon with an armful of neatly stacked shirts, slacks, ties, and a couple of suits. I was still reeling from the image of what I would look like teaching youth on Sunday morning wearing those puffy gray khakis. As I was driving home, I had a flashback to the time in college when one of my close friends warned me about what would happen if I became a Christian. "You'll lose your creativity," she had said. "You'll become homogenous."

I thought, Oh God, no … this can't be happening!

As I was driving, I began to pray a prayer of desperation, hurt, and confusion. I was hurt knowing that people in the church were talking about me behind my back. I was hurt knowing that people thought I wasn't trustworthy because of my hairstyle and clothing. I was hurt that I had actually gone out and cut my hair. And I was hurt that I was wearing clothing that I didn't like. I was crying out to God, Is this really what it means to belong to the church? My emotions were raw, mixed up, and I was on the verge of crying. It may sound silly to be so upset by something like this, but I was at such a vulnerable point in my life and in my new faith as a Christian.

Then, suddenly, I felt this incredible wave of emotion come over me. In the midst of my praying, embarrassment, and confusion, I experienced a physical sense of calm and confidence. I can't quite explain it, but it felt like someone had turned on the heater in the car and the coldness had suddenly become warmth. I had a strong sense of peace realizing that God wasn't primarily concerned about my hair or my clothing. Deep in my gut, I knew that Jesus did not really care all that much about my appearance. He was concerned about my heart, what was happening on the inside.[37] I remembered a passage I had read in the Bible: "The LORD does not look at the things people look at. People look at the outward appearance, but the LORD looks at the heart."[38] As I remembered this truth, I knew what I had to do.

I pulled my '66 Mustang onto the highway, drove straight to the Goodwill store, got out of my car, and dumped the pile of clothes the pastor had given to me onto the counter. Except for the puffy gray khakis. I considered tossing them in the dumpster as an act of mercy, not wanting to curse anyone with the misery of wearing them in public. But then I realized that perhaps somewhere out there was someone who would appreciate them. So out of sympathy for all of the lovers of puffy gray khakis, I left them there on the counter with the rest.

## THE HIGHER THE HAIR, THE CLOSER TO GOD

Looking back, it's a bit odd that my pastor never asked me why I wasn't wearing the clothes he gave me. I was incredibly nervous about it, and spent several weeks preparing my reply. But he never did ask. Maybe the haircut was enough to satisfy him. As it turned out, he left that church about six months later, and I ended up never having to explain myself to him.

Eventually, my pompadour grew back, and I haven't changed it since. Often, people ask me why I wear a pompadour haircut and why I keep it so high. There are two reasons. For one, I keep the cut because I still love the music and the style of the '50s and the fashion of the musicians I admire and respect. I know that we all have differing opinions on hairstyles, but I value the freedom of creative expression and believe that expressing our diversity and creativity should be personal and fun. Who gets to decide what makes a haircut normal? God created us in his image, and he is the ultimate designer. So why should Christians default to homogeneity instead of creative expression of all kinds?

Not long ago, I saw a painting by an artist in the rockabilly scene. She had painted a man with a very high pompadour haircut, and underneath the painting read, "The Higher the Hair, the Closer to God." I like to joke that high hair serves as a prayer antenna that helps us hear God more clearly than those with short hair, so God must approve of high hair more than short. But joking aside, the truth is that it doesn't matter how short or long or high anyone's hair is; it doesn't affect anyone's standing before God. We'd better be careful not to judge people in ways the Bible tells us not to. The second reason I keep my pompadour is to constantly remind me never to judge someone by their appearance, because I remember how I felt when someone judged me.

Sadly, in addition to my experience, there are many stories of people who have been judged and wounded by Christians based on the way they look. I once heard a pastor at a large church make a negative statement about people who have tattoos. Ironically, when he made this statement, I was sitting next to a non-church-going friend who had tattoos. My friend turned and looked at me with a "what the ...?" look as soon as he heard the pastor's comment. Afterward, I shared with this pastor what had happened and how he had come across to my friend. He was extremely apologetic; he simply had not realized how his words might sound to someone with tattoos.

Another friend once shared with me that he attended church when he was young, but left as a teenager, never to return, because he felt the pastor used the pulpit to proclaim judgment on politicians and people who belonged to a different political party.

All of these are examples of the judgmentalism that Christians are sometimes known for, incidents that influence people's perceptions of the church. A national survey of sixteen- to twenty-nine-year-olds found that 87 percent think Christians are judmental.[39] I once helped conduct a local survey in which college students were asked to share what comes to mind when they think of Christians. The most common response was "judgmental." But when we asked those same students to share their impressions of Jesus, they said "loving," "peaceful," and "kind." Something is amiss here.

## FINGER-POINTING PREACHERS

I recently typed the word *preacher* into an online image search engine. The results were fascinating. Over and over, the images I saw showed a pastor standing, speaking to a crowd, often with a stern look on his face, pointing a finger in the air. The images reminded me of the posture of someone scolding or pointing out wrongs. Recently, I showed a sequence of these images to a group of pastors I was speaking to. When I got to the image of John Travolta that I had slipped in with the rest, I joked that perhaps the roots of the finger-pointing pastor posture can be traced to John Travolta in *Saturday Night Fever* with his white disco suit and his finger pointed straight up in the air. I wish it were that simple. Instead, I fear that these images fairly accurately portray how those outside Churchland generally see many Christians: as judgmental, finger-pointing people.

The trouble with all of this is that Jesus spoke out against judging others and jumping to conclusions about people's motives, actions, or beliefs. In the New Testament book of Matthew, Jesus tells his followers, "Do not judge."[40] This may be one of Jesus' most well-known sayings. But if it's clear that Jesus didn't want his followers to go around judging others, why is the church today so well known for doing exactly that? As I continued my adventure in Churchland, I dug a little deeper into the Bible and discovered a little twist in Jesus' teaching on judgment, something that surprised me.

# CHAPTER EIGHT

# JUDGING LIKE JESUS

> This year, or this month, or more likely, this very day we
> have failed to practice ourselves the kind of behavior we
> expect from other people.
>
> — *C. S. Lewis, Mere Christianity*

JUDGMENTAL KX;

**I WAS SITTING IN A COFFEEHOUSE** not long ago and overheard
an animated conversation between two college students sitting at
the table next to me. I kept hearing phrases like "those judgmental
Christians," "they are brainwashing their poor children," "evangelical crazy fanatics," and "these innocent kids will grow up to be
judgmental." After a minute or two, I gave in and eavesdropped on
them as a learning experience. It was just too intriguing for me not
to listen in. (And they were quite loud anyway.)

I learned that the girl was upset at her neighbors, who happened to be Christians. Since they were neighbors, she had gotten
to know their children a bit. She was telling her friend that because
their houses were right next to one another, she often could hear
the parents talking in their back yard. She frequently heard them
complaining about the state of the world, and she was distressed

at how judgmental their attitudes were when they talked about people who weren't Christians or about views on sexuality and marriage that were different from theirs. She also had learned that this couple homeschooled their children because they didn't want them influenced by the "evil" non-Christian world.

This student was quite passionate as she shared her concern for these children with her friend. I could tell that she truly liked them and that she seemed genuinely hopeful that they wouldn't grow up to be judgmental and negative like their parents. I didn't say anything. But as I listened, I grew discouraged, wishing that I didn't have to keep hearing people say the same things about judgmental Christians.

A week later, I was in a supermarket and I saw the girl from the coffeehouse standing in the checkout line. I confess that I was tempted to walk over to her, put my hand on her shoulder, look up into the air like I was receiving a message from God, and say, "Fear not, the neighbor children you're concerned about won't grow up to be judgmental. Jesus says he will take care of them." But I didn't. Although I kind of wish I had, just to freak her out and see how she would have responded.

## WHAT DID JESUS REALLY SAY ABOUT JUDGING?

What I really would have liked to share with this girl is that Christians are not supposed to be judgmental in this way. There are many Christians who do not judge others like this, who are kind, loving, and accepting of other people regardless of their appearance, background, or beliefs, and I hope people don't dismiss Christianity just because some judgmental Christians fail to live it out.

Once, I was getting my hair cut by a young mother, and she shared how she had decided to keep her six-year-old daughter away from Christian churches because she didn't want her daughter being influenced by negative and judgmental people. She had grown up in a church herself, but she had experienced a culture of criticism and negativity there. So while she wanted her daughter to have some sort of spiritual upbringing, instead of taking her to a Christian church, she was now teaching her daughter Buddhism. She felt that Buddhists were more loving than most of the

Christians she had met. I found this incredibly sad and ironic. It was ironic because Jesus spoke out quite strongly against the very thing that led her to reject Christianity.

When Jesus said, "Do not judge, or you too will be judged,"[41] he was speaking to the crowds of people who had come to hear him teach, but it's likely that he also had in mind the religious leaders of his day. Many times in the Bible we read about how Jesus confronted the religious leaders and challenged their understanding of God. These were often leaders who judged others with a self-righteous attitude, looking down on people who did not align with their system of beliefs and opinions. In one encounter with the religious leaders, he accused them of making superficial judgments based on outward appearances.[42]

In his teaching on judging others, Jesus used an exaggerated illustration to get his point across, saying, "Do not judge, or you too will be judged. For in the same way you judge others, you will be judged, and with the measure you use, it will be measured to you. Why do you look at the speck of sawdust in someone else's eye and pay no attention to the plank in your own eye? How can you say, 'Let me take the speck out of your eye,' when all the time there is a plank in your own eye? You hypocrite, first take the plank out of your own eye, and then you will see clearly to remove the speck from the other person's eye."[43]

In the full context of his teaching on judgment, we see that Jesus wasn't telling people that judgment is wrong and bad. His point was more subtle. He was speaking out against a *wrong way* of judging others, a pattern of focusing on the faults of others while turning a blind eye to oneself. And Jesus used a humorous illustration to make his point. Just picture how silly it would be if you saw someone walking around with a large wooden plank stuck in their eye, self-righteously telling others that they had tiny specks of sawdust in their eyes and that they needed to get them out.

Jesus was saying that making right judgments begins with self-examination. He was teaching people first to examine themselves, their own motives, before assuming the right to point out the faults and problems of others. Jesus shows us that we need to be humble and recognize that we all have planks we need to deal with. Knowing that we have our own problems to work on — that we are no better than others — changes our attitude as we relate to other people. Jesus is teaching us that whenever we are tempted to pass judgment on another person, we should ask ourselves, "What plank do I have in my own eye?" Our first look should always be inward, at our own hearts and lives.

And when we do this, something interesting happens. We are forced to admit that we are in no place to pass judgment on others, not if the same standard we use to judge them is being applied to our own lives. Knowing that we too fall short, though perhaps in different ways, slows our desire ever to condemn others. Once we have examined our own hearts in light of God's truth, we may then come to a place where we can honestly and lovingly speak to others about our concerns. This makes *all* the difference

## "GOD, HAVE MERCY ON ME, A SINNER"

Jesus told a wonderful story in the book of Luke in the New Testament about two men. One man was a Pharisee, one of the religious leaders of the day. The other was a tax collector; tax collectors typically were despised by their fellow Jews and were considered to be sell-outs to the Roman occupiers. As Jesus tells the story, both men were in the temple praying:

> "Two men went up to the temple to pray, one a Pharisee and the other a tax collector. The Pharisee stood by himself and prayed: 'God, I thank you that I am not like other people — robbers, evildoers, adulterers — or even like this tax collector. I fast twice a week and give a tenth of all I get.'
>
> "But the tax collector stood at a distance. He would not even look up to heaven, but beat his breast and said, 'God, have mercy on me, a sinner.'
>
> "I tell you that this man, rather than the other, went home justified before God. For all those who exalt themselves will be humbled, and those who humble themselves will be exalted."[44]

I love this story.

Here we have two very different men. One, the Pharisee, is careful to keep up appearances and do everything right. He takes pride in his moral behavior and his religious activities. But he looks down on others. The tax collector, on the other hand, cries out for mercy and is unashamed to admit that he has failed God. He confesses his faults, acknowledging that he has wandered from

God's guidance, calling himself a sinner. His posture is one of bro-kenhearted humility. And it is the tax collector, not the religious leader, whom Jesus commends in this story. His humility is what God looks for, says Jesus, not a habit of self-righteously pointing out the faults of others.

## JUDGING OTHERS WITHOUT KNOWING THE FULL STORY

Jesus taught that our judgment of others should be done only in the way that we ourselves would want to be judged.[45] I know that if I'm the one being judged, I want whoever is doing the judging to know the full story. I want them to listen to my take on things and consider how I ended up in this situation, why I did what I did. I want them to understand my heart, my motives. I want them to have compassion. That's how I want to be judged. But that's not how we usually respond. It's far too easy to jump to conclusions.

A couple of years after I first became a youth leader in the church, our high school group had grown to the point where we had several hundred teenagers coming to our meetings every week, students from all different backgrounds. It was a really exciting time for me, as many of these students had never attended a church before.

There was one particular teenager, however, who gave me lots of trouble. He constantly disrupted our meetings by making jokes and distracting others while I was trying to teach. He would actu-ally throw things at me when I was in front of the group speaking. He'd bring in his skateboard, and during the serious moments in our meeting, he'd stand up and begin skating in the back of the room. For the most part, I tried to avoid him. Some nights, I secretly hoped that he wouldn't show up. After all, there were plenty of other students who weren't disruptive and disrespectful. I had pretty much written this guy off. Based on his behavior, I knew that I didn't want to invest my time in him.

One afternoon, I was walking in a section of town near the beach, and I saw this teenager sitting alone on a bench. I figured that he'd do his normal thing and make some sarcastic comment when I walked by. But then I saw that his head was down. Some-thing was wrong.

As I got closer, I spoke to him, and he looked up at me. That's when I saw that he was crying. I sat down next to him, and he began pouring out his heart to me, telling me how his dad had been arrested and put in jail ... again. He shared that his father had often been in and out of jail, and that each time this happened, he had to stay at his aunt's home, a woman who didn't really like him all that much. When he stayed with her, he had to sleep on the couch, and because she was often gone, he had to find his own meals. After learning that his dad had been arrested again, he had come to the beach, not wanting to go back to his aunt's house.

I sat there feeling horrible and ashamed.

First, I felt sad for this young man, thinking of all that he was going through with his father. I couldn't imagine what it was like to have a father in and out of jail, and having to live with someone else each time it happened. And then I felt ashamed of myself because I had judged him based on his behavior in our meetings, but I had never considered why he was acting that way. He never said anything to anyone in the youth group, so we didn't know his story. I had never tried to get to know him or to consider things from his point of view.

Now, sitting next to him, I saw not just a troublemaker but a hurting young man reacting to an extremely difficult situation. I saw a young man facing life on his own, not knowing where to turn for help.

That day, God taught me a frightening lesson: it's all too easy to become another citizen of Churchland, even when you've spent most of your life living outside it. I knew what it felt like to be judged by other Christians, and yet here I was, doing the very thing I hated. I had gone from being the judged one to being the judgmental one.

I won't forget that moment. It shocked me down to my bones that it was so easy to turn into the very thing I hated.

## DID JESUS TELL US NEVER TO JUDGE?

Although I've focused on how we *shouldn't* judge someone, we should also note that Jesus indicates there are times when we *should* judge. Jesus condemned the incorrect ways we judge others, but he also taught that there is a correct way to do it. Jesus himself often made judgments, determinations about right and wrong. Just a few sentences after warning people not to judge self-righteously, he tells the crowd that there are wolves in sheep's clothing[46] among them — people who look good on the outside but have wicked hearts and are leading people into ways of living that are the opposite of the way of Jesus, and doing it in Jesus' name. At another time, Jesus referred to these harmful people as pigs and dogs.[47] Jesus wasn't afraid to speak the truth, and he often spoke forcefully, especially when he saw people who claimed they were religious wounding others.

## THE CHURCH HAS IT BACKWARD

Let me make a statement that sounds contradictory: if people in the church correctly judged each other more often, the church wouldn't be known as being so judgmental.

What I mean (and this reads a bit like a tongue-twister) is that if the church would biblically judge the negative, judgmental Christians and stop them from wrongly judging others, then the church wouldn't be known as being judgmental, because the judgmental Christians stop their judging.

Let me explain. Judging rightly has to do with who is doing the judging, who is being judged, and how they are being judged. A fascinating example in the early church gives us some insight into how the church actually should judge ourselves so we can be a healthy church and not be hypocritical. The apostle Paul was a man who helped launch and oversee new churches and was inspired by God, writing almost half of the books of the New Testament. One of the churches he oversaw was in the city of Corinth, in Greece. Paul loved

> **IF PEOPLE IN THE CHURCH CORRECTLY JUDGED EACH OTHER MORE OFTEN, THE CHURCH WOULDN'T BE KNOWN AS BEING SO JUDGMENTAL.**

this church. He cared deeply for the people, and so he wrote a letter to them expressing his love and concern for their well-being. In this church, it was revealed that a son had taken his father's wife as a sexual partner. Paul writes about this in 1 Corinthians, the first of two letters to this church in the Bible: "It is actually reported that there is sexual immorality among you, and of a kind that even pagans do not tolerate: A man is sleeping with his father's wife."[48]

We don't know the details, but it appears that the church was fully aware of the problem. Paul wrote his letters in Greek, and the word he uses here is *porneia*, which is translated into English as the phrase "sexual immorality." It is a word that could refer to any and every type of sexual intercourse that was forbidden by God. It certainly covers this situation — a man having a sexual relationship with his father's wife.

Keep in mind that this was not just a rumor or some wild speculation like you might find in a tabloid. In the early church, people gathered in what are known as house churches, small communities in which they knew each other well. So when this incident happened, it was not a secret, and talking about it was not gossip. Paul would not have brought it up if it wasn't a glaring problem in the church, a situation that violated God's design for sexual relationships as revealed in the Bible.[49] This was not a case of judging something subjective like hairstyles or clothing. This was a blatant act of sexual immorality, and everyone knew it was happening.

Here, for all to see, was a relationship in the church that didn't represent the way of Jesus. In fact, it was hypocritical, because they were not living out what they themselves claimed to believe. Strangely enough, the church not only tolerated this, some of them were even proud of it.[50] So in his letter to the Corinthian Christians, Paul called them out and challenged them to address the problem. He even used the word *judgment*,[51] encouraging them as a church to confront the obvious sin and hypocrisy in their midst.

Though the church knew what was happening, they had let it slide. This wasn't just a one-time mistake, to be forgiven and forgotten. This wasn't someone telling a lie or two and later apologizing. Or someone getting drunk one night and doing something they are sorry for. This wasn't even someone with an addiction slipping back into their old patterns, only to cry out for help and accountability after realizing what they had done. This was a couple of Christians doing what they knew to be wrong, violating God's guidance repeatedly, and publicly misrepresenting Jesus. So Paul makes some very strong statements about what will happen to them if they refuse to change. If they continue to willingly and delightedly go against God's guidance, Paul says that they will not be allowed to continue participating in the fellowship (the community) and activity of the church.[52] That sounds harsh and judgmental! But let's take a deeper look.

## TAKING JESUS' TEACHINGS SERIOUSLY

Jesus taught many times that we must take his teachings seriously. He said to his followers, "If you love me, keep my commands."[53] Jesus said, "Anyone who loves me will obey my teaching."[54] The good news is that Jesus also promised us help. He told us that those who take him at his word and trust him will receive his Spirit to strengthen and enable them to keep his commands and obey his teaching.[55] Thankfully, we aren't left on our own. Even though we often fail to live up to Jesus' example, the Bible makes it clear that those who trust in him are forgiven by the grace of God.[56]

But forgiveness isn't then a free pass to do whatever we want. Being forgiven and receiving God's grace doesn't mean that we get to go out and continue to do the opposite of what Jesus taught.[57] Being a Christian means asking God to help us to delight in what is good, right, and true. We know that gossiping and telling lies hurts people, and we want to be people marked by love, not selfishness. So when we make mistakes and hurt others, we admit our failure, seek forgiveness, and humbly make amends. This is what the Bible calls repentance. It's when our hearts break because we have done things that go against Jesus' teaching.

Repentance should not be a scary word, the way some street preachers often use it. Repentance is a beautiful thing. The Bible says that when we recognize that we're going against God's guidance for our lives, but then repent, it is actually a time of refreshing.[58] God isn't out looking for perfect people. (There are none but Jesus.) He is looking for brokenhearted people who, helped by God's Spirit, humbly do their best to live a life that represents Jesus to the world.[59] It is God's grace that leads people to change. Through Jesus, all of our mistakes, failures, and instances of going against God's guidance — all of our sins — are forgiven through what Jesus has done.[60] Recognizing when we mess up and then repenting is important because people notice how we live our lives as followers of Jesus. People form their perceptions of who Christians are and of what the church is by observing our lives, both the good that we do and how we handle our messes. Too much is at stake for us not to pay attention to this, which is why Paul addressed the problem in the church in Corinth.

## SQUELCHING RELIGIOUS HYPOCRISY

When I taught on this passage in our church's Sunday gathering, I drew some diagrams on a whiteboard. I explained to our church that when we decide to follow Jesus, we are choosing to align our lives, our actions, our attitudes, and our values with Jesus' teachings and with the whole teaching of the Bible. To illustrate this, I drew a circle made up of little crosses. Then I drew dots all over the board, some inside the circle of crosses to represent those who choose to put faith in Jesus and trust in what he has done on the cross for them. Those who trust Jesus receive God's help (his grace) and begin to align their lives with Jesus' teachings. When we put our trust (our faith) in Jesus, we become part of the church, the community of his followers, a worldwide community of all those who have ever trusted in Jesus, regardless of when they lived. But along with this larger community that we call the universal church, we also exist in local churches, smaller communities with other Jesus-followers. In these local church communities, we exist as a mini family.

Paul explains to the Corinthian church that by tolerating ongoing hypocrisy, they were allowing it to spread corruption throughout the entire church community. Paul uses the metaphor of yeast to describe this, writing, "Don't you know that a little yeast leavens the whole batch of dough?"[61] In his culture, his message was easily understood. Yeast is used to cause an entire batch of dough to rise in the process of making bread. Paul uses this illustration to show how these two people's sin will affect the spiritual health of the entire church. Just as a little yeast introduced into dough will eventually cause the entire batch to rise, the actions of a few will change the culture and spirit of an entire community.

When I taught on this at our church, I drew an image representing a small infection and showed how it would fester if it were allowed to go unchecked. Take gossip, for example. The Bible makes it clear that Christians should not gossip or spread untruths and rumors about other people. Such actions are clearly hurtful.[62] If a church allows this to continue, they are disobeying the teaching of Scripture and allowing the person who is the subject of the gossip to continue to be hurt. Eventually, the failure to confront this behavior can lead to a culture of gossip in the church. A little leaven — an ongoing pattern of disobedience in one individual — eventually can impact many others in a church. If we don't take action to prevent hypocrisy, we allow the leaven to spread. Paul was telling the Corinthian church not to let ongoing hypocrisy continue.

The weird part in all of this "judging" is that too often the pattern is to judge people who are outside the church, instead of cleaning up messes inside the church. When I taught on this subject, I drew an arrow pointing from the church to the outside of it, symbolizing this pattern. I spoke about how Christians are quite comfortable talking about the moral failures of those who don't follow Jesus. But that's not what Jesus taught us to do. So I erased the arrow and redrew it pointing inward, at people within the church. As the apostle Paul reminds us, we need to focus on the hypocrisy inside the church and not point fingers at those outside.

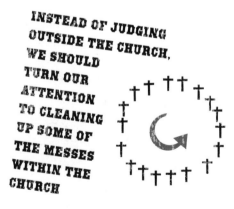

## JUDGE ONE ANOTHER, BUT NOT THOSE OUTSIDE

Paul even says, "What business is it of mine to judge those outside the church? Are you not to judge those inside?"[63] If a person has not put their faith in Jesus and committed to follow the teachings of Scripture, why should we, as Christians, expect them to live according to God's standards? Why should we expect someone who isn't even following Jesus to act like him?

Why should the church tell people outside the church how wrong they are? Finger-pointing fails to communicate grace. Paul tells the Corinthian church that judging those outside the church is a matter best left to God. He not so subtly tells them it's none of their business; it's God's role to judge those outside the church. Instead, our focus should be on our own lives and on lovingly holding other Christians accountable to their decision to follow Jesus. Judgment begins inside the church, not outside it.

If the church is comfortable criticizing the failures of those outside the church, but we turn a blind eye to gossip, pride, judgmentalism, gluttony, sexual immorality, lack of concern for the poor and needy, and legalistic living inside the church, we are hypocrites. We come to church gatherings to sing, "Thank you, Jesus, for what you did on the cross, dying for my sin," and then we knowingly continue in sin, trying to deflect attention from our problems by pointing out the flaws in others. This is the root of religious hypocrisy, and it can destroy a church community and give Christianity a bad name. That's why Paul had strong words for those who failed to confront it.

THE WORLD LOOKS IN AT US AND SEES NOTHING DIFFERENT AND EVEN HYPOCRISY. WHY WOULD THEY WANT TO BE PART OF CHURCH SEEING THAT?

HYPOCRISY

I know I am glad when friends who care about me point out when I am doing something that is not in alignment with Jesus' teachings. I don't want to be a hypocrite. I know that whenever I stray from Jesus' teachings, I need biblically informed judgment in my life, loving confrontation based on truth, not on human preferences or opinions. I need fellow Christians to help me see my flaws, but I need them to do this in the context of love.

Jesus envisioned the church as a place where people grow and change, a community representative of his grace, willing to speak the truth in love. We are all messed-up broken people who make mistakes. Followers of Jesus are simply people who acknowledge that they have sinned and are not perfect, that they need God's grace and mercy.[64] Like the tax collector, we come to God in an attitude of brokenness and humility. And that's the spirit that should characterize our churches as well. The church should be a community of people who are deeply aware of the mercy they have received, ready to share that grace, acceptance, and love with others.

Unfortunately, instead of acting like the tax collector and humbly acknowledging our need for grace, we sometimes act more like the Pharisee, looking down on others. And what do those outside the church see? A bunch of people claiming to be Christians living hypocritical lives. Why would anyone ever want to become part of our community? Why would they ever want to follow Jesus, if that's what it looks like to follow him? Some rightfully say, "The church is no different from those outside the church, and may even be worse. At least the world isn't claiming to be something it's not."

## WHY THIS IS SO INCREDIBLY IMPORTANT

In the Bible, so often we see how important it is for Christians to represent Jesus well to those outside the church. We read, "Be wise in the way you act toward outsiders. Make the most of every opportunity. Let your conversation be always full of grace, seasoned with salt."[65] In our words, through our actions, and by our example, our desire is to communicate the love and grace of God to the world around us. So when Christians act judmentally toward those who are outside the church, we need to lovingly help them stop doing that, because our reputation as the church, as representatives of Jesus, is at stake. Again, if Christians more often biblically judge the judgmental Christians (or gossiping Christians or sexually immoral Christians or Christians who ignore the poor), then perhaps we wouldn't be known in the world as being so judgmental (or as hypocrites). For this to happen, we need each other. As weird as it sounds, I know that in my life, I need to be judged.

I need fellow Christians to judge me, not in subjective things like hairstyle and clothing but when I stray from Jesus' teachings. But how we judge each other makes all the difference.

How, then, do we lovingly judge a fellow Christian?

That's what we'll look at next.

# CHAPTER NINE

# BUT JESUS SAYS... THE CHURCH IS A POSITIVE AGENT OF CHANGE

Stop judging by mere appearances, but instead judge correctly.

— *Jesus (John 7:24)*

**WE ALL ARE IMPERFECT,** broken, messed-up people. Every single one of us. When we put our faith in Jesus and God forgives us and gives us his Spirit to change us so we can follow Jesus, we must remember that we are not alone.[66] We must learn to absolutely rely on God's help daily, because we will repeatedly fail in our own strength. And God created the church, a community of imperfect people, to also help us follow Jesus. I am incredibly thankful that the church is designed for this, because we need each other.

Jesus gave his teaching to the church to help us identify areas in our lives where we are blind to our weaknesses or to the ways that we hurt others or even ourselves. A person may struggle with pride, self-righteousness, sexual sin, a habit of gossip, gluttony, or the ongoing neglect of the poor and needy. Jesus didn't tell us to ignore these things. Whenever we observe another Christian veering outside of God's standards, we need to get involved. And Jesus gives us some specific guidance for doing this: "If your brother or sister sins, go and point out their fault, just between the two of you. If they listen to you, you have won them over. But if they will not listen, take one or two others along, so that 'every matter may be established by the testimony of two or three witnesses.' If they still refuse to listen, tell it to the church; and if they refuse to listen even to the church, treat them as you would a pagan or a tax collector."[67]

When a fellow Christian strays into a habit or an attitude that doesn't align with the teaching of Jesus and we become aware of this, Jesus tells us here exactly what we should do. But first, as we looked at earlier, we should check our own eyes for planks, putting our hearts in a posture of humility and thankfulness for God's grace in our own lives. And we must remind ourselves to judge the way we would want to be judged.

## BEWARE WHEN YOU HEAR "THE BIBLICAL WAY IS ..."

It's also critical to consider whether our judgment is based on the Bible or on personal preferences. Many times I have heard Christians tell me that something is biblical when it isn't. It's their opinion, not rooted in the Scriptures. When you hear someone say, "The biblical way is ..." always check to see if the Bible really does say that. Please give anything I write in this book the same scrutiny. Well-meaning people sometimes think their opinion about something is the biblical opinion. There are certain styles of music that I really don't like but know that others do. And if I'm not careful, I can make judgments about those who like them and in my mind even think my opinion is biblical and find some Bible verses to back up why we should play only old-school gospel hillbilly music in churches (which would be my personal preference). It's a sneaky and subtle thing we can do in making hurtful judgments.

I first learned this about myself while I was dating the woman who later became my wife. I was shamefully critical because she didn't know the names of certain punk bands or rockabilly musicians. Thankfully, she did the right thing and broke up with me. She judged me to be a critical jerk, which I totally was. And to be honest, I was glad, because it helped me to take a look at myself and see just how wrong I was for doing that to her. It was a blind spot that I needed to become aware of. There is nothing in the Bible that says a person should know the name of the original bass player of the Ramones. We need to be careful not to allow our subjective opinions to become our standard for judgment. We need to study the Scriptures to make sure we accurately understand what God's guidance really is. Woe to us when we turn our personal opinions into "biblical" opinions.

> WOE TO US WHEN WE TURN OUR PERSONAL OPINIONS INTO "BIBLICAL" OPINIONS.

## APPROACH THE PERSON ALONE

After we have examined ourselves and put ourselves in the proper frame of mind, we're ready to follow Jesus' teaching. Jesus makes it clear that we should lovingly approach the person on our own. We don't gossip about them to others. We don't slander them. We go directly to them, share our concern, and listen to them, remaining open to the possibility that we are wrong. So often, taking a few moments to talk and listen will reveal that there's more to a situation than what we can see from the outside. Often, the problem ends right there.

I remember when this happened in a church I was once a part of. One of the members of our church lived about an hour from our town. One day, he walked into a restaurant and saw a man he recognized as another member of our church sitting with an attractive younger woman. He knew this man was married and that this young woman was not his wife. As he watched them talking to one another, he observed the older man reach out across the table to hold hands with this younger woman. After seeing this, he was dismayed and upset, thinking that it was clearly an inappropriate relationship. But he was careful to keep it to himself and avoid gossip.

After several days of reflection and self-examination, he approached the man and shared that he had seen him with the younger woman having what appeared to be a romantic dinner. And it was a good thing he talked with him! He discovered that what appeared to be an inappropriate relationship was actually a lunch meeting between a father and his daughter! What had looked like an adulterous touch was merely a dad reaching out to hold his daughter's hand in affection. Since his daughter lived in that town, they had met at the restaurant that day for lunch. It was a simple misunderstanding. But consider what might have happened if the man who had witnessed this had instead decided to gossip about it with some other people in the church. How might the wife of this man have felt hearing rumors that her husband was having an affair? Such accusations can be devastating, and it can be difficult to recover a reputation even when the accusations are disproven. Thankfully, this situation was handled the way Jesus taught it should be.

## UP THE LOVING PRESSURE IF THEY WON'T LISTEN

In some cases, after sharing your concern with someone, they become resistant or defensive. If this is the case, Jesus gives us a third step we can take, which is to bring "one or two others along."[68] If your concern that this person has strayed from Jesus' teachings is validated and the person resists correction, only then may you talk to one or two others and bring them to meet with the person. This shows love and respect to the offending person. It indicates that you wish to honor them and that you are not just sharing your concern with others to slander them. It's important to bring along one or two fellow Jesus-followers to confirm that your concerns are valid. If these people agree with you and the person still denies their behavior or argues that they aren't displeasing God, then Jesus suggests you raise the pressure a bit more. Bring it to the next level of community in the church, and ask them to get involved. This means going to those who know the person and asking those in their circle of community in the church to get involved to help them.

The process Jesus outlines for us is really quite healthy, loving, and respectful. This is how he teaches us to deal with those who wander from following the way of Jesus. It's a process of confronting and speaking the truth that is done with gentleness and love. Over the years, as I've been involved in church leadership, I've found that 99 percent of the time, the person confronted will see their hypocrisy and agree to change their behavior and actions. As he did with our physical bodies, God has designed a natural process of healing for his body, the church. If we are healthy, we don't intentionally hurt ourselves. The process Jesus outlines is a respectful and loving way of addressing problems that can lead to unhealthiness in the body of Christ.

However, there are times when someone doesn't want to change. In my experience, when the process outlined by Jesus is followed and a person still does not want to change, it's simply because they don't want to stop what they are doing. I recall one time when I was talking to a man in our church who was having an affair. It was a horrible situation and we were very cautious in approaching him with great humility and prayer. We did exactly what Jesus said to do, but in the end, it didn't matter. This man told us that he wanted to keep having his affair. In some cases, a person will not want to repent; they just won't want to change their heart.

This is a major problem for at least two reasons. First, it means that someone who says they are a Christian is plainly rejecting the way of Jesus. They have decided to walk the opposite way. The second problem is that their decision doesn't affect only them; it affects their family, their friends, and the entire church community. In addition, if this person continues to live in a way that is inconsistent with following Jesus, then, of course, those who look at the church from the outside will say, "Look at those Christians having affairs, or gossiping or ignoring the poor. Who are they to point fingers at us?" The health and reputation of the church are at stake. Oh, may God help us in this and guide us to be the church he wants us to be.

## AN UNWILLINGNESS TO BE UNCOMFORTABLE MEANS WE DON'T TRULY CARE

I'll admit that most of the time, I don't want to confront someone who is saying or doing things that don't align with God's guidance.

I absolutely hate confrontation of any kind. It feels incredibly awkward and uncomfortable, and my tendency is to think, "This is just between them and God. Maybe I'll just let it go. Jesus forgave them for their sins, so they can work this out with him." I'd like to turn a blind eye to these things and look past them, but that isn't what Jesus taught. If I want to follow the way of Jesus, I need to do what he says to do, even when it is something I don't like doing.

The Bible levels the ground when it says that we are all sinners. This means that we all make mistakes. None of us is perfect. No one is without fault.[69] We all have planks in our eyes and constantly need to ask God for help. But God often uses other people to help us. We need people who love us enough to tell us when we're heading in the wrong direction. This is one of the beauties of the church community. In the church, we stand side-by-side with each other, each one in need of the other, helping one another walk in the way of Jesus and seeking to represent him to the world. We do need each other to tell us when we're off, when we wander, when we are hurting others. We do need to make judgments, but out of absolute love and care for each other, not out of any sense of self-righteousness.

The apostle Paul encourages us to share our concerns with one another, and he gives us specific directions for doing that: "Brothers and sisters, if someone is caught in a sin, you who live by the

## "STOP JUDGING BY MERE APPEARANCE BUT INSTEAD JUDGE CORRECTLY" — JOHN 7:24

I am incredibly thankful that those who first welcomed me to the church, Stuart Allen and the folks I met in London, did not judge me by my appearance when they first met me. If they had, it's likely I would have left the church that day and never returned. We must learn to stop judging wrongly and learn to judge correctly, as Jesus taught us to. We all need good judgment and the willingness to speak the truth when needed. But we must do it in a way that communicates God's love and concern for those caught in bad patterns; when we do so, we help to prevent messes before they happen and restore people to right relationships with God and with other followers of Jesus. This isn't legalism. It's love.

Spirit should restore that person gently. But watch yourselves, or you also may be tempted. Carry each other's burdens."[70]

The Scriptures indicate that the reason we make a judgment and share it with someone is because we want to see that person restored. We restore a person by helping them realign their beliefs with the truth taught in the Scriptures. And we do this gently, with respect, and also with a cautious awareness that we might also be tempted in the midst of sharing our concern. I love this verse because it is a helpful warning, reminding us that we should never, ever think we're morally better than anyone else. We can easily fall into temptation and end up doing the very same thing.

## WHEN NOT JUDGING MEANS NOT CARING

This might sound contradictory, but when we fail to judge others in the church as Jesus taught, we show that we don't really care about them or about the people they hurt, and that we care more about ourselves and our desire to avoid a difficult conversation. And when we allow other Christians to go on misrepresenting the way of Jesus, we also show that we care more about ourselves than those who are not yet Christians, who then see the hypocrisy in the church and form negative impressions of the church and Christians.

It takes great courage to talk to someone about an area of weakness in their life. So when someone lovingly shares their concern about an area in my life, I try to be thankful. I try to remember that this person actually cares more about me than those who don't come to me with their concerns. Those who see my faults but claim it's not their place to judge are just allowing me to continue in damaging, unhealthy patterns. Whether they realize it or not, that means they don't care about me, those I might hurt, and the reputation of the church. We all need people who will care enough to lovingly judge and address issues in our lives when we go against the teachings of Jesus that we committed to.

I remember talking to a pastor who had to resign because of a major moral failure in his life. I will never forget what he said to me. He said he wished that when people in his church started suspecting what he was doing, they would have asked him about it. He said he even hinted at it once by subtly joking about it in a small group he was in, but no one had the courage to address it. He wasn't blaming others for what he did, but he said it might not have gone as far as it did if he had better taught his church to protect each other with "healthy" judging.

I am grateful when a fellow Christian comes to me and asks about an area in my life that seems out of sync with the way of Jesus. I know I need people around me who will tell me the truth and who want me to be the best person I can possibly be. I know that I need to regularly be "judged" or I am prone to wander from Jesus' teaching. So I've asked my friends to love me enough to tell me when I'm doing something that is wrong or when I have a poor attitude. I have given them the freedom to correct me when I'm not acting in agreement with the teachings of the Scriptures. And they do! When I begin to gossip, they shut it down and tell me to stop. When I become critical of someone and it leaks out in my words, they confront me. They tell me when I'm off, correcting my perspective so I don't drift into selfishness and pride. We all have areas of weakness, and that's why Jesus taught us not to ignore them and to involve others in helping us follow him and his teachings.

## HOPE FOR A HEALTHY CHURCH

If you are a Christian, know that other Christians need you to help them faithfully live out their calling as God's people. You are needed. We are all in this together. The church is made up of messy people, and we must make every effort to help each other follow Jesus by holding each other accountable to his teachings in the way he taught us to — in love and grace. Whenever the life and words of someone you care about do not align with Jesus' teachings and the Scriptures they claim to believe, you must speak up. It's the way Jesus set up his church to function in a healthy way. And if you are not a Christian, I hope that you understand better why there is sometimes hypocrisy in the church and judgmental Christians who incorrectly judge others.

I love the passage in the New Testament letter to the Galatians where the apostle Paul tells us that "the fruit of the Spirit is love, joy, peace, forbearance, kindness, goodness …"[71] And in his letter to the Colossians, Paul describes how Christians should act:

"clothe yourselves with compassion, kindness, humility, gentleness and patience."[72] My hope is that one day Jesus' church will be known for the things that Scripture says should characterize his followers. When someone is asked to describe Christians, instead of saying "judgmental," they will say, "I don't share all their beliefs, but they certainly are a people of love — kind, peaceful, gentle, and patient." I truly believe this can happen.

> **You have heard it said ...**
> The church is judgmental and negative.

➡

> **But Jesus says ...**
> The church is a positive agent of change, loving others as he would.

## BEYOND JUDGMENTALISM

One Sunday evening, I saw a young couple standing outside the doors of our building as people were coming in for our evening worship gathering. I was puzzled. I had already seen them earlier that day at our morning gathering. Why would they come again in the evening? They weren't serving in any official way during the service, so there was no need for them to be there.

So I asked them what was going on.

They shared how that morning, after our gathering, they'd gone downtown to have lunch. As they were walking downtown, they saw a small group of Christians holding large signs with flames and fiery red letters that read "Repent. Judgment is coming." Other signs listed various sins. This group stood on the street corner to attract attention, and as people walked by, they did the stereotypical thing, shouting that people were sinners and would be judged by God.

As this couple watched, they noticed that most people either ignored the street preachers or were irritated by them. Many of them had gone downtown to shop or hang out for lunch, and now they were being confronted by signs about hell and by people they didn't know who were shouting at them. This couple decided to approach the group to find out where they were from and learned that they weren't even from our town at all. The group had just thought it would be good to drive to our town to share what they felt would help people want to follow Jesus.

Now I should be clear that I don't disagree with their message, for the most part. I believe that one day God will judge everyone, just as the sign said.[73] But what's the most effective way to communicate that message? Is it standing downtown, shouting at strangers while holding signs with flames on them? I believe this only reinforces stereotypes that Christians are judgmental, and it communicates that the primary message of the church is negative.

My friends gently suggested to this group with the signs with the flaming letters that there are already many churches in our town that care for people and are trying to share the wonderful news about Jesus with them. They also shared their sense that this particular approach wasn't very helpful to the local churches' ongoing mission. They were sincere and respectful as they shared their concerns, but this group didn't seem to care. They were convinced that their confrontational and impersonal sign-holding way of telling people about Jesus was the right way — and the only way.

Again, this couple are very restrained and soft-tempered people. I've rarely seen them worked up about something, but this interaction set them off and led them to do something contrary to their normal introverted character. They left the group of street preachers, went to the art supply store down the street, and bought some poster board and several thick markers. Then they created signs that said things like "This isn't all that Jesus talked about" and "Jesus is about joy in this life too." They took the signs and stood right next to the group of street preachers, just to show people there was another message, an alternative to the one they were hearing.

And something amazing happened.

While the other group, with their flaming signs and shouts, was basically ignored, people began to read these new signs and several stayed to talk and ask questions. All afternoon, this couple had conversation after conversation with different people about Jesus, the church, and the Christian faith. They provided a different approach, and people responded. So the reason the couple was back at church that evening was to follow up with several people who had expressed an interest in coming to the church worship gathering that night. This couple wanted to be there at the door to greet those they had talked with that afternoon and welcome them to the evening gathering.

Stories like this give me hope that the church will one day be known as people of kindness, grace, humility, and love, not as judgmental and condemning. We don't have to change our theology or lessen our sense of urgency to proclaim who Jesus is and about salvation through faith in him.[74]

But I long for the day when I can sit in a coffeehouse and hear a girl share how she's really impressed with how loving and kind her Christian neighbors are. Or hear that the hairstylist will want to bring her daughter to the church because she knows it is a place of love and will be a good influence on her child.

This won't just happen. We who are Christians must take steps to break the stereotypes. As I was exploring church and Christianity, I was so relieved to discover that Jesus did not tell his followers to be judgmental and negative. He did say to lovingly judge and help restore other followers to a healthy place, but that's a far cry from being judgmental and condemning.

After I better understood the question of whether Christians are judgmental, I needed to address the question of whether contemporary Christianity is nothing but an "organized religion" and not what Jesus wants it to be. And as with the question of judging others, I discovered some surprising answers.

# CHAPTER TEN

# YOU HAVE HEARD
## —IT SAID...—
# THE CHURCH
## ★ IS AN ORGANIZED ★
# RELIGION
## —THAT—
# CONTROLS PEOPLE

I don't think there's anything wrong with the teachings of Jesus, but I am suspicious of organized religion.

— *Madonna*

**THE COFFEE** that splashed from my cup and onto my hand was pretty stinking hot. My friend and I were in the midst of a fairly heated discussion about Christianity. She'd been inquiring about my newfound interest in Jesus and was genuinely concerned for me. To her, Christianity wasn't a positive thing and was an organized way of imposing ideas on others, an institution responsible for inciting war, fear, and division. Based on her experience with Christians, she believed that Christianity was about overly restrictive rules and dogma imposed on people by controlling leaders. She believed the church taught that to be acceptable to God, you had to pray a certain way, believe specific doctrines, and conform to the political agenda and preferences of the church.

And so she presented me with several objections to organized religion, things she had noticed about the church and many of the Christians she had observed over the years. I fumbled a response to her objections as best I could, but for every explanation I offered, she had even more objections to share. Finally, in frustration, and out of genuine concern for my future, she slammed her hands on the table, inadvertently splashing coffee on my hand, and shouted with great emotion, "Danny, don't you understand? Christianity is organized religion! Religion is the opium of the masses!"

I vividly remember that moment, and not just because my hand got burned by the coffee. Her statement was burned on my mind as well.

As you likely know, my friend was referencing Karl Marx's statement about religion being the opium of the masses. Marx was a German philosopher, a political economist, and a social revolutionary. He is often called the founder of modern communism. When my friend shouted at me, she was thinking of Marx, who used opium as a metaphor for religion. Opium is a pain reducer, a mind-numbing drug that can also be quite addictive. And Marx saw in it a fitting metaphor for religion because he believed that organized religion was simply a way for those in power to control others. It was a pleasant drug that allowed people to avoid the real pain in their lives. It numbed the mind so that people no longer had to think for themselves. Marx believed that Christians had checked out intellectually, numbing themselves with religious ideas and allowing church leaders to control them.

And now my friend thought I was becoming one of them.

But was it true? Does Christianity numb the mind? Is organized religion simply a means of controlling people? Were her concerns justified?

## THE CHURCH OF SIMON SAYS

Another friend recently shared with me why she isn't part of a church anymore. The biggest reason is her sense that the church is just an organized religion; she prefers to seek God with more freedom than the organized church allows. She told me that the last time she went to a church meeting, it felt to her like a game of Simon Says. The leader onstage told everyone when to stand up and when to sit down, when to clap their hands, and what phrases to repeat. Having studied the Bible a bit, she didn't recall seeing any of these activities in there, but this church was organized a certain way and had strong preferences for certain practices and for the way they wanted people to act. She felt forced into this pattern of doing exactly what the leaders wanted, sort of like she was playing Simon Says. She confessed that she felt more connected with God out riding her mountain bike on the trails than in this forced religious experience.

Another friend shared with me how he dislikes that some churches seem to organize themselves around certain political views. As a teenager, he attended church with his parents and could remember their pastor consistently bringing up the hottest political issues when he spoke from the pulpit. To him, it felt like the pastor was trying to play another version of Simon Says, encouraging people in the church to vote a certain way on the issues he felt were important. His sermons were a way of controlling people to align with his personal political beliefs. The way this pastor spoke and acted led my friend to believe that if a person in the church disagreed with the political views being taught, the church would no longer accept them or welcome them in the community. This left a strong impression on him, and my friend has not visited a church since his teenage years. He wants nothing to do with the "mind control" of organized religion.

## WHAT IS ORGANIZED RELIGION?

So what do people mean when they use the phrase *organized religion*? This objection to the church is so commonly repeated, but it's not always clear what people mean when they use it. I once posted a question on my blog asking people

**OR·GA·NIZED:**

*adj.* 1. Having a formal structure, as in the coordination and direction of activities. 2. Efficient and methodical.

what they mean when they refer to the church as organized religion.[75] Some of the responses included:

- "Organized religion is when the church becomes controlling and doesn't allow people to question or think for themselves."
- "Organized religion doesn't give birth to anything: its purpose is to assimilate existing organisms into an efficient, controlled, and predictable structure. The bureaucracy exists for itself, and although its actions may benefit others, its primary purpose is to preserve and control itself."
- "Organized religion is when the church dictates what you do with God. They tell you how to pray, when to pray, how to sing, when to do this or that. If you question what the church does, then you're a bad person. There is freedom in Christ, but the church boxes Jesus into an image of who and what they think he is rather than allowing some freedom."
- "The 'church' (or other entity) exists to further the organization itself (buildings, money, power, hierarchy, etc.) rather than creating a movement for the good of the world."
- "Organized religion is when the church turns into a machine replete with systems, structures, strategies, mission, vision, values, culture, procedures, goals, objectives, core beliefs, systematic theology, policies, checks and balances, staff manuals, due diligence, legal, financial, and denominational oversight.... Would you like me to continue? I know what it's like ... I once ran it."

The definitions people shared describe the church as a controlling institution that dictates the how, when, where, and what of a person's relationship with God. The organized religion of the church tells you how you should worship God and how you should pray. Some believe that the church has systems in place to control how people think about truth or theology, all in an attempt to conform people to a specific way of thinking. Others suggested that the organized religion of the church is all about systems of leadership and means for establishing control and retaining power over others.

There is some validity to all of this. I remember the church meetings I attended in my college years and how they had restrictions — things you could and could not do — and thinking that the meetings felt a bit forced at times. One group was "organized" by pressuring you to clap your hands and sing upbeat songs that sounded like commercial jingles. Another was "organized" in a way by using droning organ music, men wearing strange robes, and the repetition of unusual phrases spoken in unison.

> **RE·LI·GION:**
>
> *n.* 1. A set of beliefs concerning the cause, nature, and purpose of the universe, often containing a moral code governing the conduct of human affairs. 2. A personal set or institutionalized system of religious attitudes, beliefs, and practices.

Now that I've been involved in the world of the church for some time, I understand that these different ways of doing things depend on various traditions, and I can even appreciate them in a way that I didn't at first. When I began my adventure in the world of Churchland, all of this was just plain confusing and not too appealing. I was searching for God, and it felt like people were trying to force God into their own little boxes, conforming God to their own subjective preferences and opinions. It felt like church was even divided into so many subchurches all claiming to know what God is like and what it means to be a Christian. This became more pronounced to me when I started looking for a church and practically got dizzy seeing how many said this is the way church is supposed to be.

## PHONE BOOK CHURCH SEARCH DIZZINESS

As I shared earlier, when I returned to the States after my time in London, I knew it was important to find another church so I could continue growing as a Christian. Not knowing where to look, I turned to the phone book. (This was in the days before Google.) And as I looked in the yellow pages under "churches," I was quite overwhelmed. The church section went on page after page after page. It was broken down by different types of churches, and some of them had some very weird sounding names. Words like *Presbyterian* and *Episcopalian* reminded me of the names of different strains of viruses. I had no idea what they meant or even how to pronounce them. Some of the church names had state names in them, like Lutheran Church Missouri Synod. I assumed this was a church for Lutherans who were from Missouri. (But what's a Lutheran?) It was all very confusing.

The church I attended in England was called Chapel of the Opened Book. It was a pretty simple name, easy to understand. The "opened book" refers to the Bible, so it was simply a place where people gathered to open the Bible and learn.

Looking at the long list of church names in the phone book, I knew I was in trouble.

I found Evangelical Lutheran Synod churches, Lutheran Church Missouri Synod churches, Evangelical Free churches, Free Methodist churches (each time I saw the word *free* in a church name, I wondered if it was because the others charged an entry fee), United Methodist churches, Presbyterian Church in America churches, Presbyterian Church USA churches, and on and on. There were churches that called themselves Christian Reformed, United Reformed, Dutch Reformed, Greek Orthodox, Russian Orthodox, United American Baptist, Conservative Baptist, Southern Baptist, Reformed Baptist, Anabaptist, Seventh-Day Adventists, Disciples of Christ, United Church of Christ, Church of God, Church of God in Christ, Assembly of God, Church of the Nazarene, Salvation Army, Foursquare Gospel, Plymouth Brethren, Mennonite, Quakers, Vineyard, Episcopalian, Anglican, Catholic, and Calvary Chapels. Some churches were even categorized as nondenominational, and I wasn't sure why they didn't belong with any of the others.

As if it weren't difficult enough trying to understand all these different types of churches, what made my phone book church search even weirder was that some of the churches in the yellow pages ads seemed to be competing with the others, as if they were businesses. There was a slogan indicating that a church was "the friendliest church in town" (and the others weren't?), and several made it a point to use the word *relevant* in their slogans — relevant preaching, relevant music, and so on. Some of the ads also used phrases like "we have a *rockin'* band." I found it fairly odd for a church to describe their band as rockin'. I figured that if they had to tell me their band was rockin', it likely wasn't.

All of this got me thinking: would the early Christians ever have guessed that in two thousand years there would be all these divisions in the church? If a first-century follower of Jesus were alive today and he went looking for a church in a phone book or did a Google search, what church would he select from the list?

## WHY CHURCHES ORGANIZE AND DO THE THINGS THEY DO

As I was venturing into Churchland, I experienced a constant tension in my life. I had read enough of the New Testament to know that being a follower of Jesus means being connected to a community of other Christians. And my experience in the London church had given me a taste of how wonderful Christian community could be, so I knew that what I had read was true and good. I knew that I needed a church, a community of other followers of Jesus to belong to.[76] But I was put off by strange-sounding denominational names. I had no idea how to tell the difference between all of these subgroups of Christianity. I knew that I didn't want to get involved in a cult or a closed-minded fundamentalist group or the scary churches you see in movies that dance around with snakes.[77] I also knew that I didn't want to belong to a group that wasn't interested in wrestling with questions, thinking about what they believed and why.

So I decided to do some research.

Why were there so many different churches organized in all these different ways? And how were they different from one another? I knew that I had to take seriously the concerns some of my friends had about what they feared were the mind-numbing effects of organized religion. So I read some church history and began to understand that much of what happens in a Sunday church meeting is not necessarily required by or even mentioned in the Bible. It's often a way of organizing and of relating to one another that is based on personal preferences, habits, and traditions that developed at a particular time and in a specific culture. In fact, when you study church history, you discover that several things we assume are normal today were not part of the early church.

**1. The early church did not have official church buildings for their weekly meetings.**

The early church we read about in the Bible typically did not meet in a building designated exclusively for religious purposes.

There was no stained glass, no pews or pulpits. For the first three hundred years, most believers simply gathered in their homes.[78] Some of them led and taught the others, but they all were united as a community of people who had come together to follow Jesus and serve others. As the church grew in size, some of these house gatherings eventually did move into buildings dedicated for that purpose. But this was not, in itself, a bad thing. Growth is a natural, normal part of life. It happens organically. And it *should* be normal if God is indeed changing people's lives and more and more people become followers of Jesus.

Today, people might still gather in a home, or they might choose to meet in a special church building, a school cafeteria, or a movie theater. It doesn't really matter where we meet. It's what we *do* that matters. Not just on Sundays, either, but how we live during the other days of the week. The early church gathered in homes where they shared meals and worshiped God together through teaching and singing. These meetings were informal, but they were still structured to facilitate teaching and praying together.[79] So having church buildings and organization are not the problem. In fact, they can be good and helpful things. But I never realized that for several hundred years, the church mainly met in homes.

I remember talking with a twenty-four-year-old man who was visiting a church for the first time. He had brought some coffee with him into the sanctuary — the room where the people were gathering to sing and hear a message from the pastor. As he entered the room and sat down, some ushers came over and informed him that coffee was not allowed in the sanctuary. He shared with me that this experience was really embarrassing for him, as several other people saw this confrontation, and it made him feel like an outsider. While there may have been valid reasons for banning coffee in that room (not staining the carpet?), we should remember that the early church served meals and drinks when they met, so having a coffee in a worship gathering certainly is not unbiblical. [80]

When carpets or buildings become more important than people, a church begins to reek of organized religion. The Bible never makes the church building, where believers gather, into a sacred, magical place. It's just a building. And we need to be careful that we don't organize our church around our building. Instead, we organize our building around what best helps us to faithfully follow Jesus and make a positive difference in the world, even if we suffer a few coffee stains on the carpet.

**2. The early church's buildings did not reflect the design of Roman courts or Broadway theaters the way today's churches often do.**

After learning why the early church moved out of homes into bigger buildings, I began to understand why churches also had to become more organized. There is a difference between a gathering of thirty or forty people and a gathering of hundreds or thousands. I found that when the church moved from homes into formal buildings, they first modeled the design of these buildings after structures that were common at the time — Roman basilicas, which were government courtrooms. Many of our church buildings today still use this architecture. They were rectangularly shaped, with a stage at one end of the building. In a Roman basilica, you'd find those who were speaking separated from the rest of the crowd, elevated and up-front, facing the people.

In the 1300s, pews were added to church buildings. These became especially important after the Reformation started in the 1500s and the sermon became the focal point of Protestant church meetings. People now needed to sit down to hear a longer message or teaching. The Bible was placed on the podium, similar to where the books of Roman law were placed in basilicas. Where once there was a judge presiding over the court, now you'd find a preacher. And though we are far removed from the days of Roman law, this design still impacts the atmosphere of our meetings, whether we're aware of it or not.

Today, not all church buildings still follow this style. Now you can find buildings with sloped floors, comfortable theater seats, and lights that illuminate the preacher and the musicians on a stage. In the nineteenth century, the design of many churches changed from the style of a Roman courtroom to the architecture of the theater. This was done to aid in communication and reflected changes in the culture.[81]

I've been to several churches whose building was originally set up like a Roman law court with pews and a big pulpit in a long building, and they changed it. They took out the pews so they could set the seats differently. Some smaller churches even put couches in the sanctuary so it truly does feel more like what an early house church community might have been like. It's interesting that somone who is used to a traditional Roman law court type of setup might be confused or even upset seeing such a casual church meeting space, when actually the casual living room feel was more of what the traditional early church was like. Even most large churches today that are too big to set up their sanctuaries differently have smaller midweek meetings in homes.

I find it fascinating to think about why churches do what they do. To be clear, there's nothing wrong with any of these buildings. The Bible is silent on the type of building we use for gathering together. There is no one right way to design a church building. The problem is not with a particular type of building; it's when we get locked into organizing ourselves around a single style of architecture and begin to think that the way we do things is the biblical way. It is sad when Christians waste time arguing over what size or type of building our meetings should be in. When we prioritize our preferences over God's mission of seeing as many people as possible learn who Jesus is, we run the risk of becoming an organized religion.

### 3. Communion was celebrated differently in the early church.

I didn't limit my study of church history to the changes in buildings and architecture; I also wanted to know if the practices of the church had changed over time. I thought about the Cup of Wonder, as my friend Randy unforgettably called it, that Christians drank from in memory of Jesus' death on the cross, and so I studied the history of what is now commonly referred to as communion, the Eucharist, Mass, or the Lord's Supper. I learned that originally, this practice was not a distinct act where a church leader served people a small piece of bread or a wafer and a small cup of juice or wine. Instead, it was included as part of a full meal that the early churches ate when they met together in houses. The bread the early Christians ate wasn't just a thin wafer or a small Chicklet-shaped cracker. The cup was actually a full glass of wine, served as part of the meal, not the grape juice we drink out of miniature plastic cups served in trays after being blessed by a church leader.[82] In other words, we practice this celebration meal quite differently from the way it was originally practiced.

There are many ways of celebrating the Lord's Supper in the church and even various beliefs about what happens when we eat it and what it means. It was refreshing to me to take a look at why we do what we do. Studying the history of the Lord's Supper reminded me that this isn't just an empty ritual. Whenever we do something over and over again, there is a danger that we will lose the meaning behind what we do and become organized in an unhealthy way, forgetting why Jesus instructed us to do it in the first place.

**4. Sermons today are different from the way Scripture was taught in the early church.**

As the church moved into larger, more formal buildings, the pulpit and the preacher were elevated higher than the other people of the church so they could be seen and heard. Over time, the church also adopted a more Greco-Roman approach to communicating and teaching. These changes led to a greater sense of separation between the leader and the people of the church. To be clear, the Bible does teach that the church should have leaders and a leadership structure.[83] Again, there is nothing necessarily wrong with having a person stand on a platform. When I teach at our church, I stand on a raised stage. The Bible does not dictate what style we should use when we preach or whether we should stand on a raised stage or preach from behind a pulpit. What matters is if the Bible is being accurately taught and if people are able to understand and act upon what they hear.

The Bible can be taught in a variety of ways. Some churches today have artists who paint while the sermon is being preached. As a visual learner, I totally appreciate these visual elements. But the fun thing I discovered from the Bible itself is that we have a lot of freedom in how we teach. There are many different ways to organize a message to effectively communicate the teaching of the Bible. But if our particular methods become the "right" and "biblical" way and we criticize those who preach differently than we do, we've become organized religion. If we care more about our style of preaching than whether people are learning truth from the Scriptures and are responding to what God says, then it's likely that we've become another organized religion.

**5. In the early church, church leaders dressed no differently than other people.**

Where did all those strange robes come from? And why do so many preachers wear suits and ties today? Over time, church leaders began dressing differently than the common people of the church. They felt that certain clothing would help them better fulfill their mission in the culture they lived in. In the Roman Catholic Church, leaders borrowed from existing fashion designs and created unique clothing to distinguish their leaders. During the Reformation in the 1500s, church leaders decided that they would wear the clothing of a scholar — a robe. Wearing a robe meant that your pastor was educated and gave an additional sense of authority to his teaching. Today, the only time you see someone wearing a robe like this, outside of a more formal church setting, is at a graduation ceremony or in a courtroom.

There are good reasons why people choose to wear different types of clothing, and some church leaders choose to wear clothing that meant something in the past (such as a robe), even if today most people have no idea why they wear it. In more formal churches today, you'll often see the leaders wearing suits and ties. Again, there is no biblical mandate for this; it is simply felt to be a way of showing respect for what they do, a way of honoring God. This can still be confusing to people. For some, a church leader wearing a suit and tie on a Sunday appears dignified and elicits respect for their role in the church. Yet to others, the suit and tie represents the world of business and politics, a culture that they do not typically associate with religion and spirituality.

For the first several hundred years of the church, people just wore whatever they had to church gatherings. There was no special clothing for church. Most often, they met on a Sunday night, since Sunday was a workday, and they gathered for a meal and a time of teaching and prayer, and then they used the bread and wine they had left from the meal to remember Jesus together. (This was their communion or Lord's Supper celebration.) It's doubtful that they dressed up or put on different clothing for this meeting.

Even many of the formal titles we use today for church leaders — words like *reverend, minister,* and *pastor* — were not used in the Bible. You never see someone in the Bible saying "Hey, Reverend Jim." And while certain people had the role of pastoring, the role of guiding and caring for a group of people, there's no indication that they used these role descriptions as official titles.[84] Formal titles for church leaders developed later, and again, while there's nothing wrong with using them, it's just another tradition based on preferences, not based on the Bible itself. When a church allows titles and dress codes to get in the way of its mission, it is in danger of becoming an organized religion.

I was amazed to learn about the rich history of the church and how it developed over time. I once assumed that the way churches did things was exactly what was taught in the Bible, and my study of the early church and the history of Christianity was very helpful. I learned to appreciate the diversity of methods and styles that people have used to express their worship to God, and it helped me to see that Christians aren't all homogeneous and uniform in their practices. I learned to enjoy this diversity: being in more formal churches, less formal churches, big churches, small churches, house churches, all kinds of churches. But as appreciative as I am, I can still see why some don't like the Simon Says approach if a church becomes too organized and restrictive, and teaches or models that their approach is the only right and biblical way.

## THE CHURCH OF THE SHOE-BOX SIZED CAR PHONES

When I came to see that there wasn't a biblical basis for many of the things that I had found confusing about the church, it was quite a relief. Most of the things that had confused or troubled me when I first encountered the church were simply a matter of tradition, not biblical requirements. A tradition can be a practice or way of doing things that originated in 1505, 1925, or even 2005. Traditions develop whenever a church or institution does something that proves to be quite helpful, and they continue to do it again and again. Good, healthy traditions continue to have a clear purpose and meaning, and they reinforce what the church believes is true and important. But some traditions continue to be practiced long after the reason for doing them has been forgotten, and they may not make much sense anymore.

I remember a scene in an '80s movie on television in which a man was using a car phone. The movie was filmed when car phones were new, and so the phone was gigantic. It looked to be about the size of a shoebox. It was humorous to see him holding it to his head

*Eric Risberg/AP Images*

as he talked. There was even a coil that ran from the phone to the receiver in the car, since it wasn't wireless. You couldn't just walk off wherever you wanted with the phone, since the antenna was connected to the car itself. You had to stay in or near your seat to use it.

At one time, this car phone was cutting-edge technology. It served a clear purpose in its time, helping those on the road communicate with others. But now, thanks to improvements in technology, we've found much easier ways to communicate. We now use smaller wireless phones instead of giant shoebox-sized ones wired to a vehicle.

Wouldn't it seem a bit strange, though, if we were still required to use those giant car phones because they were once useful during a specific time period? Or if we claimed that the large shoebox-sized phones are the traditional way of using a phone, and so we shouldn't change that tradition? Or if we resisted change that is helpful for the church and even argued and fought about it when it is all really just our preference and not based on the Bible?

I was once given a copy of a letter that was written by a church member to a music leader in the church who was trying to change the musical style of the worship service. It read, "I am no music scholar, but I feel I know appropriate church music when I hear it. Last Sunday's new hymn — if you can call it that — sounded like a sentimental love ballad one would expect to hear crooned in a saloon. If you insist on exposing us to rubbish like this — in God's house! — don't be surprised if many of the faithful look for a new place to worship. The hymns we grew up with are all we need."[85]

You might assume that this letter was written recently, but the irony is that it was written in 1863, and the song this person was so concerned about was the hymn "Just As I Am." Today, that hymn is considered a classic and is sung in many different churches around the world. Yet when it was introduced into the church, people were upset. It was different, a change from what they normally sang. Sadly, the person writing this letter had organized their religion around a particular style of music and felt threatened by change.

## BRINGING IN THE ORGAN AND THEN KICKING IT OUT

Another example of this that I find fascinating is the organ. For centuries, many churches used an organ as their primary instrument of worship. When people suggested that the organ was outdated and didn't connect with people anymore, many in the church fought back. How dare they even think about taking the organ out of the church? But what's humorous about this (unless you happen to love the organ) is that when you look at the history of music in the church, the church resisted ever bringing the organ into the church in the first place. It was considered a pagan instrument, used for signaling the entry of kings and queens. Many felt that it was an unthinkable sin to bring an instrument like that into the church.

Of course, as with many things, over time the organ was not only accepted, it eventually became the most common instrument in the church. Now we are in yet another time of transition. As more churches decide to remove the organ and use contemporary instruments, it often causes tension and fighting in the church. So we fought to get the organ into the church, and we fight to take it out again, and it's all just personal preference. The organ isn't even mentioned in the Bible. It didn't exist at the time the Scriptures were written.

## FREEDOM AND CREATIVITY IN ORGANIZING THE CHURCH

When I speak to church leaders, I often say to them, "If tradition gets in the way of mission, it is sin." We have to be careful that we don't put tradition or the way we do things so high on a pedestal that we value that more than people. Instead, we should be concerned about whether people are truly learning from Scripture, whether they are connecting with God and worshiping and experiencing community together and experiencing love, whether people who don't know Jesus are coming to learn about him and follow him. Those are the questions we need to be asking.

The truth is that we have great freedom in the church to organize how we meet. We know that in the early days of the church, there were some things that all the churches did. They had meetings — both large and small — typically in homes.[86] They usually met on a specific day of the week called the Lord's Day, the first day of the week. The Bible indicates that when Christians gather, there should be teaching from the Scriptures. There should be prayer. Jesus' followers should care for each other, meeting each other's needs. They should regularly celebrate the Lord's Supper together and should baptize new believers.[87] There should be leaders whose responsibility is to care for people.[88] But apart from that, the Bible gives us a lot of freedom for structuring our church meetings, as well as freedom to decide how to dress, what music to use, how to set up the room, and whether to have artists painting during our worship gatherings. Christianity is not bound by practices or traditions that are limited to a particular time or culture, and the church can be a beautiful, flexible, ever-changing community of creativity.

So what does Jesus think of all the energy we expend bickering over something like an organ? Well, Jesus might not have had to worry about *that* particular problem. But we do know how he responded when he encountered organized religion in the temple.

It wasn't pretty.

# CHAPTER ELEVEN

# ANGRY JESUS
## — WITH —
## ★ ★ A WHIP. ★ ★
## — FREEING —
# BIRDS

I'm not into organized religion.

*— Neil Young*

Organized religion is a sham and a crutch for weak-minded people who need strength in numbers.

*— Jesse Ventura*

There are things about organized religion which I resent. Christ is revered as the Prince of Peace, but more blood has been shed in his name than any other figure in history.

*— Frank Sinatra*

**I HOPE** I never find myself being chased by an angry, whip-carrying Jesus.

When I think of Jesus, I picture him sitting peacefully on a grassy hillside teaching people to love their enemies.[89] I see Jesus

The Buyers and Sellers Driven out of the Temple, by Gustave Doré (1832–1883)

calmly and gently reminding people that they should love their neighbors as themselves.[90] Or I have an image in my mind of Jesus tenderly reaching out his hand and healing people.

I don't typically think of him running after people, red-faced and angry, brandishing a leather whip and flipping tables. But that is what Jesus did one day on a visit to the temple. The story is told in the New Testament book of Mark: "On reaching Jerusalem, Jesus entered the temple courts and began driving out those who were buying and selling there. He overturned the tables of the money changers and the benches of those selling doves, and would not allow anyone to carry merchandise through the temple courts. And as he taught them, he said, 'Is it not written: "My house will be called a house of prayer for all nations"? But you have made it "a den of robbers."'"[91] John, one of Jesus' disciples, also records this event for us in John 2:15, and John adds that Jesus "made a whip out of cords" to chase the money changers away.

Now, as I read this story, I can imagine what it might have been like to be there in the temple courts that day. You hear commotion near the money changers. So you turn to see what's happening, and you see a fuming Jesus running full force with his hand raised, holding that whip. He looks really angry, flipping over tables, scattering cages of doves to the ground. As the doves fly away, free from their cages, you suddenly see Jesus running straight at you, whip held high. I know what my first thought would have been. "Oh #&@! (whatever phrase they would've used then) Here comes Jesus! And he is really, really mad!"

I'd probably faint if I had been there that day and seen Jesus coming after me like that. It's a scene that seems so strange because it appears to contradict so much of what we read about the life and teaching of Jesus in the New Testament.

So what caused Jesus to get this upset?

## ORGANIZED RELIGION THAT RESTRICTS WORSHIP GETS JESUS MAD

When we take a closer look at the unusual way Jesus responded here, we learn that the cause of his being upset was organized religion. Jesus was visiting the temple courts in ancient Jerusalem that day. At that time, the temple was the central place where the Jewish people gathered for worship. The Hebrew Scriptures (the Old Testament of the Christian Bible) gave clear guidelines for proper worship in the temple. For example, there was a specific order to the sacred functions of the priests and an established rhythm of daily and weekly worship, as well as special festivals throughout the calendar year. Those who believed in the God of Israel came to the temple to worship God at set times of the year.

While this organization might seem confining to us today, these regular patterns and rhythms were actually good things, creating a celebrative experience for the people, one that had deep meaning for them as they remembered God's love and his faithfulness to his people. It must have been amazing to see people from all over the known world, of different backgrounds and ethnicities, gathering in Jerusalem — men, women, rich, poor, young, old — all coming together to worship God.

The people needed certain things in order to experience the festival and offer their sacrifices, and since they were things they could not carry with them while they travelled, they had to purchase them upon their arrival in Jerusalem. And to make these purchases, they needed to exchange their foreign money into the local currency. So we need to remember that the money changers were providing a necessary service, helping those who were visiting Jerusalem to participate in the festival. The exchanging of money and selling of objects needed for sacrifices in the temple wasn't in itself a bad thing. That's not why Jesus was angry.

## TURNING THE BEAUTY OF WORSHIP INTO THE UGLINESS OF SEGREGATION

As Jesus was overturning the tables and chasing people with a whip in his hand, he quoted a passage from the Hebrew prophet Isaiah.[92] This gives us our best clue as to his motives. The passage from Isaiah speaks about the worship of God at the temple, stressing that it is to be a place of prayer for people of all nations. But that wasn't happening. Jesus was angry at the religious leaders because they had turned something beautiful, a vision for a multiethnic community of worship, into an organized religion. The religious leaders had determined what the appropriate rules for worshiping God were, rules that went beyond what the Scriptures taught. These rules were their personal opinions, and they were changing the way God's people worshiped.

The religious leaders had organized worship by segregating the different areas in the temple by race and gender to ensure proper "purity." Jewish women were allowed to enter only at a lower level than the men, and non-Jews were limited to the outermost court. There were also restrictions that prevented anyone who was blind, lame, deaf, or mute (even children) from having full access to the temple. The "house of prayer for all nations" — a visible sign of unity — had become a system of segregation and a visible sign of division. Human rules and restrictions had led to blatant discrimination.

That's why Jesus was so incredibly angry and even used a whip.

Jesus also quoted the Hebrew prophet Jeremiah[93] when he accused the religious leaders of turning the temple into a den of robbers. In Jeremiah, we see God condemning the Jewish leaders for using the temple as a hiding place for criminal activity. Jesus was implying that the religious leaders had allowed the temple to be used for organized crime and personal profit. He accused them of taking advantage of the people's needs. The beauty of the temple had been tarnished by greed and power. A place of worship was turned into a place of segregation and profit making.

## IS IT TIME FOR THE WHIP?

Though it's easy for us to condemn the religious leaders of Jesus' time, before you start celebrating their whip-cracking punishment, consider this question: if Jesus were walking around Churchland today, would he bring another whip and do some chasing in our churches? I see nothing wrong with churches that have coffee, CDs, and other items available for sale in their buildings provided the goal isn't for big profit and taking advantage of people. But if Jesus were visiting churches today, would there be any he'd find just as guilty of turning something beautiful into a system of organized religion that controls people? Have any of today's religious leaders turned following God into a culture of oppression and conformity, where questions about truth are suppressed and political agendas are promoted in the name of Jesus?

If so, perhaps it's time for Jesus to dust off that whip.

I can say pretty assuredly that most churches don't set out to control or hurt people. And most don't. But it does happen. Over time, churches can change and begin to place a higher value on their systems and programs than on the people they are called to serve. These systems can be anything from the way they run their Sunday meeting to the process they use for making decisions. It can be the way the leadership in a church is chosen or how members join. Whatever the tradition is, if that tradition becomes more important than the mission of seeing people come to know Jesus, then it's time for the whip.

But it's not just the traditions of the church that can be problematic. Sometimes the church organizes itself in a way that embraces a particular agenda or political party. We shouldn't try to suggest that Jesus was a Republican or a Democrat. Jesus wasn't interested in building a political party; he called people to an entirely different party — the kingdom of God.[94] When his fellow Jews tried to make him an earthly king, Jesus refused.[95] Jesus was not naive about the political dynamics around him, and he was clearly aware of the plots and plans of those opposed to his mission. Yet Jesus chose not to fight on a political level; he went directly to the people. His goal was to transform society not by changing the political system but by transforming the human heart. Whenever we confuse kingdom priorities with partisan politics, it's time for the whip.

Finally, while I know that most churches aren't into mind-control, the truth is that in Churchland we can sometimes unintentionally create a culture that discourages critical thinking and asking questions. A youth pastor once shared with me that his church would not allow him to read books by authors who were not aligned with the theology of the church. This pastor was not an antagonistic person and spoke gently with a high regard for the other staff. Because he couldn't even raise questions for fear of losing his job, he confessed that he had created a secret bookshelf in his home because he feared losing his job if any of the other staff members saw the books he was reading. It's terribly sad when churches create a culture where people feel compelled to hide what they are reading and are afraid to ask sincere questions. Eventually, this young man left his position at this large church, a church that seemed to be quite hip and open to new music and contemporary décor but didn't encourage people to ask theological questions. When the beauty of the church as a place to explore theology, raise questions, and learn is marred by unhealthy control and suspicion, it's time for the whip.

## EMBRACING DOCTRINE DOES NOT MAKE YOU CLOSED-MINDED

I won't deny that I hold some very specific theological beliefs and strongly embrace what some would call the historic doctrines of the Christian faith. I would gladly defend these beliefs and even die for some of them. But just because a person has strong theological beliefs doesn't mean they have been sucked into an unhealthy form of organized religion. The truth is that we all have some type of organization to our beliefs. If you are married, then you have certain beliefs about what it means to be married, beliefs that organize the way you act and think as a married person. When you pursue a particular career or vocation, you need to have organized beliefs to be able to do your work effectively. A chef in a restaurant has certain organized beliefs about how food is cooked. A doctor has organized beliefs about practicing medicine. Even someone who says they aren't into organized religion has organized beliefs about why they don't like organized religion. This is completely normal.

So when a person decides to follow Jesus and begins studying his teachings and learning what the Bible says about life and God, it is only natural to develop some organized beliefs. And that's exactly what Christians have been doing since the time of Jesus. There are certain beliefs that Christians have held through the centuries that reflect what is taught in the Bible. What I mean by "historic doctrines of the Christian faith" are ones like those expressed in the Apostle's Creed and the Nicene Creed. Doctrines such as believing that Jesus was crucified on a cross, that he died, that he was buried, and that he rose from the dead after three days.[96] Christians believe there is only one God.[97] They believe that the Bible reveals this one God in three persons: the Father, the Son, and the Spirit.[98] They believe that this God created everything that exists.[99]

Christians also believe that Jesus' death was a substitutionary sacrifice for sin, that Jesus died so that sinful people could be forgiven and given new life.[100] And they believe that following Jesus means sharing the message of what he has done with other people and taking loving action to promote justice and compassion.[101] These are just a few of the historic beliefs of the Christian church, doctrines that most churches have held and taught for the past two thousand years.

The fact that churches have core convictions and beliefs doesn't mean that they are trying to control the way people think. Nor does it mean that Christians are closed-minded. Some Christians might be closed-minded, but the overwhelming majority aren't. It is possible to have organized beliefs, yet do so with humility and reverence.

## HUMBLE THEOLOGY

I like using the term *humble theology* when I speak of doctrines and my organized beliefs. Holding a humble theology means that we approach the Scriptures with an understanding of our inadequacy as human beings to grasp with certainty every single thing that is taught in the Bible. But living with a humble theology doesn't mean that we should live without beliefs and convictions. There are many doctrines that the Bible teaches, doctrines that have been held throughout the two-thousand-year history of the church and whose truth and clarity we can have confidence in. Doctrines are actually good things, although the word often is associated with negativity. This word *doctrine* simply refers to teaching or instruction, beliefs that can be taught and learned. The Bible itself tells us to "watch your life and doctrine closely."[102] I love that the Bible says that it's not enough just to pay attention to what we believe — our doctrine. It also reminds us that we must also watch our lives —

that we should live our beliefs. Doctrine is meant to change our lives, not just be head knowledge. Our organized beliefs should melt our hearts so that we become more like Jesus.

## DOES HAVING ORGANIZED BELIEFS MEAN THAT WE SHOULD NOT STUDY THE BELIEFS OF OTHERS?

What I have learned to love about Christianity is that embracing specific doctrines and even organized beliefs about God does not prevent us from continuing to be in constant dialogue with other people, exploring the variety of opinions on a topic and hearing what others have to say. Whenever we respond with fear to beliefs that differ from our own, we reveal a lack of confidence in what we believe. Was Jesus afraid to interact with those who disagreed with him? We see one example of his approach in his interaction with the Samaritan woman at the well, as he discusses worship with her.[103] Jesus corrects her errors but treats her with respect. We also see this type of interaction modeled by the apostle Paul in the book of Acts.[104]

In my library, I have books written by Bible scholars who don't believe that Jesus rose from the dead. I even have books by Satanists (Anton LaVey's autobiography). I don't agree with what these authors believe. In fact, some are entirely in opposition to my convictions. But I read these books to learn how people who disagree with me think and how they arrive at their conclusions. Reading books like these — in addition to the many books that clarify, express, and affirm what I do believe — helps me when I talk about my faith.

In the church I belong to, we all agree on certain core, historic doctrines and beliefs. But we also have differing opinions. For example, all of us believe that Jesus is going to return one day to earth as he promised his followers.[105] But exactly how and when that will happen is a matter of some debate. There have been various opinions on this throughout church history. We all agree that God created everything that exists. But we have differences of opinion about whether this happened in six twenty-four-hour days or over the course of six billion years, or whether this debate misses the point entirely by misreading why Genesis chapter one was written.[106] So while we all agree on the majors — the core biblical doctrines that Christians have held for two thousand years — we also have differences of opinion on the minor areas of belief.

## "IF ONLY CLOSED MINDS CAME WITH CLOSED MOUTHS"

I understand that Christianity is generally thought of as an organized religion, which to most people usually means dogma and doctrines not to be doubted or questioned. But the good news is that Christianity isn't really like that. In the New Testament, people in a city called Berea questioned the teaching about Jesus that they had heard from the apostle Paul. So they went to the Scriptures to study it for themselves. Was this frowned upon? No, they were called "noble" for their earnest search for the truth.[107] God commends questions as people seek truth. Yes, Christianity has organized beliefs. Jesus had organized beliefs. But we can look at more than two thousand years of church history to how these organized beliefs have made a difference in people's lives.

One of my favorite characters in the Bible is Daniel, whose story we read in the Hebrew Bible. Daniel was taken from Jerusalem into captivity in Babylon. Daniel was trained in Babylonian philosophy and even was given a new name, *Belteshazzar*. (The "Bel" part of his new name came from the Babylonian god Bel.)[108] Did Daniel freak out? No. Instead of refusing to learn new things, he discerned the activities that would lead him to compromise his worship of the one true God, and he drew his lines there. Though he refused to pray to and worship anyone other than his God, Daniel was not afraid to live in a foreign, pagan culture. He remained strong in his faith in the God of Israel, even while immersed in the world of the Babylonian gods. Daniel's example shows that you can remain open and active in a culture that is radically different from your own, while still remaining faithful to your convictions. God used Daniel to make a difference in Babylon because of his discerning actions. It is important to note that Daniel held to his theological convictions, but he didn't close his mind while doing so.

Like Daniel, Christians, of all people, should be open-minded learners. We should constantly work to stretch our thinking outside our own faith, while not abandoning it. That's what Daniel did. This is important because Christians can be known as closed-minded nonthinkers. But Jesus sure seemed to want his followers to be thinkers. He shared stories through parables that required people to use their minds. Jesus also taught people by asking them questions.[109] So when we hear of churches or Christians who discourage those who ask questions and show an interest in thinking critically about their faith, it's a sign that organized religion has taken hold.

There is a bumper sticker that says, "If only closed minds came with closed mouths." It's a humorous dig at people who like to make their dogmatically and rigidly held opinions known to others, perhaps referring to some obnoxious Christians. But as we have seen, those who follow Jesus should keep their minds open to hearing and exploring new ideas and opinions and asking questions.

> ## IF ONLY CLOSED MINDS
> ## CAME WITH CLOSED MOUTHS

Being open-minded does not require you to believe that everything is truth, nor does it necessitate abandoning the essential historic truths of the Christian faith. If you have experienced restrictive thinking and have found it difficult to raise questions about Jesus and the teaching of the Bible, please know that there are many Christians who love to dialogue and explore questions about their faith while still retaining a commitment to the historic beliefs of the Christian faith.

Biblical Christianity truly does encourage thinking, asking questions, and using our minds. Finding this out was such a relief to me, because from the outside looking in, I had thought differently. In fact, when I explored the big question about whether the church is just an organized religion that wants to control people, I found that, while it sounds contradictory, organized religion actually has some very positive aspects, which I'll explain in the next chapter.

# CHAPTER TWELVE

# BUT JESUS SAYS... THE CHURCH ★ IS AN ORGANIZED ★ COMMUNITY THAT SERVES PEOPLE

Religion that God our Father accepts as pure and faultless is this: to look after orphans and widows in their distress and to keep oneself from being polluted by the world.

—*James 1:27*

**THE PHRASE** *organized religion* almost always is used negatively. When I first was exploring Christianity, my plans were that if I discovered that it truly was organized religion, then I wouldn't be part of it. Yet to my great surprise, I learned that Jesus was actually into organized religion. But not like we may think.

Not all organization in a religious setting is evil or wrong. Organization need not be forced; it can often be organic, as in the way the body organizes itself in the process of development and growth. When thought of this way, organization isn't all that bad. It simply means there's a structure in place to coordinate activities for efficiency. We see the benefits of organization all the time. Watch a sports game and you will see how organization is necessary for the teams to play fairly. Go to a school and you will find everything organized for training and teaching students. Visit a hospital and hopefully you will find an organized method for treating and healing people. We all hope that our bank accounts and financial records are organized so we can keep track of our money.

But organization can also have a dark side. Nazi Germany was organized. Terrorists can be organized. We talk about organized crime. And we must confess that historically, the church has been organized for some terrible reasons: religious wars, racism, and oppression. We need to learn from this if we want to reclaim God's vision for the goodness and beauty of the church. There are ways of organizing religion and having an organized church that can be healthy and helpful and bring honor to Jesus' name.

## A HEALTHY FAMILY IS ORGANIZED

Think of the church as a family, which is one of several metaphors the Bible uses to describe the church.[110] A family is relational and organic, but a healthy family needs a certain level of organization, ways of operating that allow it to function efficiently. Someone must be responsible for preparing the meals. Someone has to pay the bills. There must be schedules for sleeping and for waking up for school or for work. Chores are divided up. Healthy families plan times for work and for rest and schedule time to relax and hang out together. Husbands and wives set aside time to be alone together. The unavoidable truth is that for any relationship to be healthy, it must have some sort of organization.

What makes the difference between healthy and destructive organization is what you are organizing for. When the church decides to organize around controlling people, politics, and self-preservation, it eventually leads to unhealthy and restrictive organization. But when the church organizes around the biblical mission that Jesus gave his followers to share his good news of hope and forgiveness with people and lovingly encourage them in their desire to know Jesus, this leads to healthy organization — organizing ourselves to serve others. We can organize the church for acts of goodness such as caring for the poor and helping those in need. We know that this type of organized religion actually pleases Jesus.[111]

## JESUS PRACTICED ORGANIZED RELIGION

It seems like a clash of philosophical values to think that Jesus approved of organized religion. Even using his name and organized religion in the same sentence seems like trying to mix oil and water; it grates like the sound of fingernails on a chalkboard. But Jesus was into organized religion — of the right kind.

Religion is merely having a set of beliefs which shape and govern the way we live. You could say we all have a religion, because we all have beliefs. Whether Christian or atheist, we have beliefs which influence our lives and how we live.

Jesus was religious and practiced organized religion. He went to synagogues and to the temple in Jerusalem.[112] He observed the Jewish celebration of Passover and other Jewish holidays.[113] Jesus kept the Law — the first five books of the Hebrew Bible — and studied the Scriptures. All of these things were part of highly organized religion.

But when organized religion goes against the teachings of Scripture, is corrupted by power or greed, and hypocrisy is the norm, this is organized religion that Jesus hates.[114]

So Jesus was very "religious," and he established an organized religion (in the good sense of the term) when he established the church.[115]

## THE ORGANIZED CHURCH THAT JESUS WOULD BE PLEASED WITH

Jesus himself was organized. When he was preparing and training his followers to launch the church, he modeled for them an organized pattern in his prayer life. Luke 5:16 tells us, "But Jesus often withdrew to lonely places and prayed." And he taught them to observe the organized religious practices of the Lord's Supper and baptism.[116]

Jesus used the metaphor of a vine when he talked about his followers. He taught that he is the vine and his followers are the branches.[117] Yet even something organic like a vine needs organized care for it to grow in a way that produces healthy grapes. Vines are grown on trellises, structures built so they are lifted off the ground, and they need irrigation systems. So Jesus' metaphors about his followers would have included ideas about structure and organization.

Another metaphor commonly used in the New Testament to describe the church is the image of a body.[118] The apostle Paul uses this metaphor to illustrate how the various parts of a human body are organized so that they all function together for specific purposes. A hand can't function like an eye or an eye like a hand. And that's the way he says it should be in the church as well, all of the diverse parts coordinating to function organically, yet organized. The New Testament also teaches that there is organized leadership for the health of the church.[119] Just like our bodies have parts and systems that are organized to keep our bodies healthy, the Bible teaches that the church has leadership roles and systems designed for keeping the church healthy.

We read in the New Testament that the early church grew and eventually needed to change the way they were organized. At first, the church was small enough that the structure was fairly loose. But eventually, as the church continued to grow, many of the widows in the community were being neglected.[120] A better organizational structure was needed to make sure the widows were properly cared for. So the early church changed itself, becoming more organized to help it fulfill its mission.

When organized religion organizes around the things Jesus would be pleased with, amazing things can happen. Over the years, the church has organized to serve and help others in many different ways:

- Christians were organized in the early church to help meet the needs of the widows, the orphans, and the outcasts of society.[121]
- In the fourth century, Basil of Caesarea and John Chrysostom of Constantinople organized the church to construct orphanages to care for infants and children who had no parents.[122]

- During the Industrial Revolution, William Booth organized the Salvation Army to feed, clothe, and provide shelter for people in need.
- Christian leaders in the 1800s organized to have several bills passed in England to protect children against abuse. At that time, children as young as five years old worked more than sixteen hours a day in coal mines and fabric mills.
- In the late 1800s, a Christian politician, William Wilberforce, organized a campaign for the abolition of slavery. His efforts led to the freeing of seven hundred thousand slaves and the abolition of the slave trade in the British Empire.
- Today, numerous evangelical Christian ministries, such as Compassion International and World Vision, are organized in partnership with the church to raise millions of dollars to support children and families in need all across the globe.[123] These Christian relief agencies are often some of the first groups to help in global emergencies like earthquakes and floods. These groups also organize the ongoing support of several million children through child sponsorships. Each month, sponsored children receive financial help, and sponsors write letters to them to develop an ongoing relationship with them. Millions of children would lack the food, education, and relational connection they need without the aid of these organized religious ministries.

Just last night I had dinner with my good friend Rick McKinley, who is a pastor in Portland, Oregon. He has helped to organize a church program called the Advent Conspiracy,[124] an annual Christmas campaign that encourages Christians to spend less money on themselves and more on helping those in desperate need around the world. Several thousand churches join this mission every year and have raised millions of dollars to bring relief to people in need.

> "RELIGION THAT GOD OUR FATHER ACCEPTS AS PURE AND FAULTLESS IS THIS: TO LOOK AFTER ORPHANS AND WIDOWS IN THEIR DISTRESS AND TO KEEP ONESELF FROM BEING POLLUTED BY THE WORLD."
> — JAMES 1:27

Another friend of mine, Allison, who is a devout Christian and part of a church, serves on staff with several other Christians in the Not for Sale Campaign. They have organized a global effort to end human trafficking and slavery.[125] At our church, a successful businessman named Nathan was constantly haunted by the poverty he saw in his travels around the world. He eventually quit his job and started a company called to promote fair trade practices that help support people in need all over the world.[126] He makes various fair trade products available for sale in the United States while working to solve some of the systemic problems that cause global poverty.

At one fair trade event that Nathan held at our church, I purchased a cross that had been made in war-torn Liberia out of the spent bullet casings that litter the ground everywhere. These crosses were made by those whose families were killed in the Liberian civil war. Every time I look at it and remember where it came from, this small cross serves as a powerful symbol of hope and peace. It's a symbol of Jesus handcrafted from an instrument of death, a reminder of transformation from hate to hope, from death to life. The event made thousands of dollars to help those in need, and our church was educated about these needs around the world.

These are just a few examples, and there are hundreds and thousands more out there who are doing similar things. But in all of these, it is because Christians and churches are "organized" that beautiful and good things happen. I believe this is the type of organized religion Jesus is pleased with.[127]

## ORGANIZED RELIGION IS THE HOPE OF THE MASSES

I still get embarrassed about the ways the church has sometimes become the sort of organized religion that Jesus wouldn't approve of. But I am also very encouraged by the fresh wind of change in the church today. Some of the negative press about the church is understandable, but what is often missing is reporting that communicates all the good things the church has organized to accomplish for the good of others. And that sometimes gets forgotten when people criticize the church. Without downplaying the wrongs that have been done by the church, we also need to acknowledge the many things that the church has done right.

In recent years, a number of bestselling books have been published characterizing the church as an organized religion which is destructive, hateful, and a cause of war and death.[128] Some of these books point out all the terrible things done in the name of God or of Jesus Christ. I won't deny that terrible things have occurred, but we must remember that these acts were not the result of people following Jesus' teachings. They are clear deviations from his teachings. There will always be those who claim to be acting on behalf of God while doing the very things that God hates. Just because something is done in the name of Jesus doesn't mean that Jesus approves.

There is something else to consider when some loudly claim that organized religion (especially Christianity) is the source of most of the evil in this world. When we consider the evil that has been committed and the wars that have been perpetrated by those who claim no religion, it's not hard to see that the record is equally bad, if not worse. In recent centuries, there actually have been more wars incited and terrible social evils committed by those who claim no religion than by those who do.[129] In fact, historical studies have shown that more than 93 percent of all the wars in human history had no relation to religion.[130] For example, Joseph Stalin was an avowed atheist who wished to see Christianity purged from existence, yet he was also responsible for the killing of more than ten million people under his Communist regime.

I was recently having a drink with a passionate atheist friend who was using the very common argument that organized religion is to blame for all war and hatred. I was able to reverse the tactic and share these statistics about how much war and murder can be blamed on those who claim no religion. He got silent for a minute and then said, "It's still wrong when organized religion does it," to which I said, "I totally agree." And Jesus would not approve of it either. But don't just blame organized religion when atheists and those who claim no religion have done the same, if not worse, in human history.

If I can offer a twist on that famous quote by Karl Marx, I would suggest that far from being the opium of the masses, organized religion is truly the hope of the masses. When the church gets organized around the things Jesus cares about, great things can happen. When Jesus pulled out his whip and began chasing people in the temple, he was opposing organized systems of division that prevented those who were seeking God from truly worshiping him. But Jesus encouraged an organic yet organized structure for his followers and gave them a vision of becoming his body: his arms, feet, and hands in the world today, working together and doing what he instructed his church to be doing. We are to be representing him, telling others about him and his message. The church doesn't exist only for itself. It is an organized community on a mission to serve people.

> **You have heard it said ...**
>
> **The church is an organized religion that desires to control people.**

→

> **But Jesus says ...**
>
> **The church is an organized community on a mission to serve people.**

As I travel around the country, what gives me so much optimism about the church is that I see that so much is changing. When the organized church avoids the negative aspects of organized religion and instead focuses on being organized around the things Jesus taught and the mission he gave, that organization brings people hope and life. It's an incredibly beautiful thing to witness. This is why organized religion can be hope for the world. Just think of the amazing things that God has done through the church that represent Jesus well, such as helping abolish slavery, fighting against human trafficking, and caring for the poor around the world. The potential is incredible as the church organizes itself to bring about exponential change in the world.

If you're not yet following Jesus and confess that you dislike organized religion, I truly don't blame you for feeling that way. Or if you were part of a church that strangled the life from you somehow, I understand, because I also had some bad experiences. But I hope that you will consider what I am saying and take note of the majority of Christians and churches, some which are probably in your own community, that are not like the ones that are organized for control or power. Instead, they are organized by truly following Jesus' teachings, and they desire to serve people and make a positive difference in others' lives.

For those who follow Jesus, this is why the church needs you and your unique giftedness, creativity, and contribution to Jesus' mission of serving others and teaching them the good news of who Jesus is. There's too much need in the world not to be part of the organized church. We all are to be part of bringing about change, helping the church to be the "organized church" the way Jesus intended and would be pleased with.

## PART THREE

# GRACELAND

# CHAPTER THIRTEEN

# ESCAPING
★ ★ CHURCHLAND ★ ★

I have become comfortably numb.
— *Pink Floyd, "Comfortably Numb"*

**I WILL NEVER FORGET** the innocence and joy I had when I was
first getting to know Jesus. If you are a Christian, perhaps you can
remember how it felt when you studied the Bible for the first time.
Everything was so new, alive, and unbelievably refreshing. For
me, living in London and being mentored by Stuart Allen, really
studying the Bible for the first time, was an incredibly wonderful
period when my faith came alive. It was a time when my faith felt
adventurous. I say that because when you believe that the Bible is
inspired by God and that it's true, it's a thrilling and vulnerable
state to be in.[131] By faith I eventually believed that what Jesus said
about himself is true. A sense of awe accompanied my realization
that God loves me, that I am completely forgiven and accepted by
God through Jesus because of what happened on the cross.[132]

So it was quite difficult to leave London after spending a year
there playing in the band, not just because I would miss London and

the fun of playing music but because I would miss Stuart Allen and my church family. Stuart and that tiny little church of elderly people had given me hope that I might fit into the church, after years of thinking it was impossible. They made me confident that it's possible to be a Christian with intelligence. They ignited my heart to serve other people and care about those who don't yet know Jesus. Stuart also equipped me to continue my study of the Bible on my own.

Before returning to the United States, though, I decided to take a detour. I didn't have to head back right away because after the band ended our year in London, I had no job to go back to. So I packed up my bags and headed to Israel to live on a kibbutz. I figured that if I was going to study the Bible, Israel was a great place to do that.

## "THANK YOU, GOD, FOR THE MATCHING SHOELACE"

When I first arrived in Israel, I travelled and saw many of the typical tourist sights. I was reading the Bible all the time, taking it everywhere I went, and I was learning the lay of the land, getting a better grasp of the geography. It was in Israel when I really began talking to God as part of my everyday experience. I didn't have another Christian to converse with, so I developed a habit of talking to God, just like I would talk with a trusted friend. I'd share what I was thinking or feeling as I walked along, having silent conversations with God.

I spent a lot of my time walking back and forth to the various biblical sites. I remember one time when I was walking to the location where it's believed that Jesus gave his most famous talk, the Sermon on the Mount.[133] On my way, one of my shoelaces broke. It had broken earlier that week, and I had tied the pieces together as a temporary fix. But now it was clear that the laces were done. I wasn't wearing any socks and was starting to develop some painful blisters, so walking was quite miserable. My foot kept slipping in and out of the unlaced shoe. Though I was having an ongoing conversation with God, it seemed like such a silly, trite thing to ask God to fix my shoelace. Finally, as I neared the base of the hill, the pain in my foot grew almost unbearable. I stopped walking, looked up, and prayed in frustration, "God, my foot hurts, and I need a shoelace!"

Nothing happened. I didn't expect it to. So I continued hiking. A bit farther down the road, I noticed a small path through some high grass off to the side of the road, a shortcut leading to a church building on the hill. I began walking through the grassy area, and after about ten feet, I stopped. There, sitting on the ground in front of me, was a single shoe. It was quite freaky because I had just prayed for a shoelace, and just a few minutes later there was a shoe. I picked it up and saw that the laces were fairly new. Not only that, but they perfectly matched the color of my shoe.

At that moment, the sun was shining, and I was standing on the side of a road near the Sea of Galilee, in the very place where Jesus himself had lived and taught. As hokey as this sounds, I lifted up that shoe, high in the air, and said out loud, "Thank you, God!" I was even pleased that God cared enough to make sure the color of this shoelace coordinated with the color of my shoe.

Now, I don't know how it got there. Was it a coincidence? I don't know. Perhaps there was an Israeli couple driving down the road and God somehow spoke to the driver, telling him to take off a shoe and throw it out the window. I can picture him, driving with his wife looking confused as she watches him pull off his shoe and chuck it right out the window.

"Honey, what are you doing?"

"I don't know, dear. I think I'm supposed to throw my shoe out the window."

It very well could have been a coincidence, but to this day I wonder if God chose to provide a shoelace for me at that time in my faith journey simply to encourage me and build my faith. All I know is that my faith and my love for God were growing every day as I studied, talked with God, and walked throughout the land of Israel. And finding that shoe that day was a little part of that.

I began developing trust with God and learning to depend on him to meet my needs. I was still very confused about different lifestyle issues, not really knowing what was right or wrong according to God's guidance in the Bible. During my time in England, I hadn't been living the most morally upright life, and the same was true during my time in Israel. But despite my confusion, I sensed that I was changing. I knew that God was changing me, little by little, and it wasn't about having to obey rules or giving in to pressure from other people. Stuart hadn't focused on any of that when we had met together in England. He had spent his time simply helping me get to know Jesus better. I wasn't changing because someone was telling me that I had to live a moral life. No one gave me a list of things I could or could not do to be a good Christian. I was changing because I wanted to change, because I wanted to follow Jesus. It just started to make sense to align my life more with what Jesus and the Bible taught as I was choosing to follow him.

## BAPTIZED IN FRONT OF A BUSLOAD OF GERMAN TOURISTS

One day, I went to see the Jordan River and was watching some people from a church in the States getting baptized. The wife of the pastor doing the baptisms started talking with me, and she asked me if I had ever been baptized. I hadn't, so after the pastor was finished with the baptisms, she called her husband over and he invited me to be baptized right then and there. I thought to myself, "What better place is there than here?" so I agreed and was baptized. I waded into the Jordan and was dunked in the water by a pastor I had met just minutes beforehand. It wasn't something I had planned to do that day. But it just felt right, and I knew from reading the Bible that getting baptized was something that Christians did when they decided to follow Jesus. My most vivid memory of my baptism is coming up out of the water and looking up to see a busload of German tourists taking photos of me. They were all lined up along the bank of the river, snapping pictures while I was being dunked in the water.

The more time I spent reading the Bible and praying, the more I sensed a fullness of life that I hadn't known before. I noticed that in addition to my own study of the Scriptures, the Scriptures seemed to be studying me. It felt like I was being asked to look at my life. The Bible was changing me from the inside out.[134] I had a growing confidence that God is real, that the story of Jesus I was reading in the Bible is true, and that the Bible itself is a very different kind of book, inspired by God.[135] It wasn't an irrational faith, because I was also reading books on the origin of the Bible and reasons for trusting that it is inspired. I also was amazed at all the archeological evidence that corresponds to the Bible stories. So my short time in Israel brought the Bible to life in many new ways for me.

And then, my touristy Bible site visits were over, and it was time to head to the kibbutz.

It was not at all what I was expecting.

## ESCAPE FROM DOUBLE DOUGH

While I was in London, I learned about kibbutzes and decided to go to one. A kibbutz is a community of people who choose to live together, sort of like a very small town. These communities were established in the early 1920s by Russian immigrants who had moved to Israel, and today they accept volunteers who work at the kibbutz for a period of time in exchange for free room and board. A lot of young Europeans go to Israel and live on a kibbutz, and I had a friend who went to one. They sounded like a fun way to spend a couple of months with other people my age while getting to see Israel.

The first kibbutz I was sent to was not at all what I had hoped it would be. It was set deep in the wooded hills above Nazareth, and as soon as I arrived, they put me to work in the bread factory. I had been hoping to do something outdoors, possibly related to agriculture, so being stuck inside in a factory was quite disappointing. Even more disappointing was learning that our work was all done from 11:00 p.m. until 5:00 a.m. Everyone who worked at the bread factory worked at night and slept during the day.

My job was to watch the bread as it rolled out of this huge oven on a conveyer belt. I wore thick gloves, and whenever two loaves were stuck together, I yelled, "Double dough!" and they stopped the conveyer while I yanked the loaves off the line. The room was super hot and loud because of all the machinery, and after working on the Double Dough line for a week, I knew there was no way I was going to spend my short time in Israel indoors, up all night, working at this bread factory. I asked my supervisor if I could transfer to a different kibbutz, thinking they'd just shift me to another location. But to my surprise he said no. They were very strict and told me I had committed to three months and that I had no choice but to stay.

Suddenly, the kibbutz seemed an awful lot like a prison.

I panicked. I knew that I didn't want to stay at the Double Dough, but I wasn't sure what else to do. So instead of showing up for work that night, I escaped. It was a bit like a prison escape, because they actually had some armed security guards and a fence surrounding the property.[136] I gathered all of my belongings into a pillowcase, climbed the fence, and fled into the woods in the hills surrounding Nazareth. It was completely dark that night, and there were no paths for me to follow, so I ended up getting lost. For several hours, I walked around in the woods trying to recover my sense of direction. At one point, I fell off an embankment, ripping the sleeve off my jacket. I had no water and no flashlight, and I was pretty exhausted after a couple of hours. Eventually, I found a dirt road and saw a house in the distance. It was very late in the wee hours of the night, and the lights were out. But at that point, I was so cold and tired that I just walked up to the front porch, wrapped the welcome mat around me, and fell asleep.

I was awakened at the crack of dawn by a woman standing over me, yelling at me in Arabic. I don't blame her for yelling; I probably scared her by falling asleep on her porch. After several attempts at apologizing, I left as quickly as I could and made my way down into the city of Nazareth. I was totally exhausted because I hadn't slept much, and I was fairly dirty from a couple of good falls I took in the woods. As I walked into town, it was still very early, and there weren't any stores open yet. I was so thirsty from my evening adventure, I found a soda machine and bought what turned out to be the most amazingly tasty orange soda I have ever had. As the sun rose in Nazareth, the boyhood home of Jesus, I sat on a curb sipping my orange soda and opened my Bible and prayed for a while.

Soon afterward, I was able to arrange a transfer to another kibbutz, where I stayed for the remainder of my three months. This was a much more pleasant experience, because I was working outside in the grapefruit fields. I was able to enjoy my remaining days in Israel, working at a sunny kibbutz, far from the noise and heat of the Double Dough.

## FROM ESCAPING DOUBLE DOUGH TO ESCAPING CHURCHLAND

Though I had successfully escaped the Double Dough kibbutz, it wasn't the last time I felt trapped and wanted to escape. After returning to the States, I eventually found myself wanting to escape again. But this time I wasn't trying to escape from a fenced-in kibbutz in Israel; I was trying to escape from falling into the comfortable subculture of the evangelical church.

> Welcome to the Jungle
> We got fun 'n' games
> We got everything you want
> Honey we know the names
> — Guns N' Roses, "Welcome to the Jungle"[137]

If you change "the jungle" to "the bubble," the Guns N' Roses song "Welcome to the Jungle" is a pretty good way of describing what my new life in evangelical Churchland was like. As I shared earlier, when I came back to the States, I found a church to be a part of, the one with the musical and the puffy pants. After I got over those experiences, I settled into life in another church, and a strange and unsettling thing happened to me. Without realizing it, I slowly became immersed in this new subculture. But this subculture was different from the small group of elderly people in England. Unlike the church in London, where we had nothing more than an old organ, dated pamphlets, and some foldout card tables in the basement, there was a dizzying array of books, music, toys, and trinkets in the American evangelical church world. I found that whatever I liked to do, there was a "Christian alternative" available for me. If I liked golf, there were Christian golf balls and golf tees with Bible verses on them. If I liked coffee or tea, the local Christian bookstore sold Christian tea bags with Bible verses printed on them and Christian coffee mugs with Christian sayings.[138] There were Christian concerts, Christian music festivals, and special Christian days at amusement parks. It was quite a cultural shock. Until then, I had no idea these things existed.

But the surprisingly weird thing that happened was that all of these comforts and resources made it very easy for me to quickly lose some of the dependency on God I'd had when I was on my own. In England and Israel, I often cried out to God, desperate for his guidance and help (or a new shoelace), but after becoming immersed in this new Churchland subculture, I found that I didn't do that as often as I used to. Ironically, as I got more and more involved in church, my life became so filled with Christian activities and new Christian friends that I lost the dependency on God that I had in England and in Israel. I'm embarrassed to say that I became more and more comfortable in evangelical subculture.

I'd attend church meetings on Sunday and hang out with my Christian friends. I'd go to a Bible study on Tuesday night and hang out with my Christian friends — again. Then, I'd go out Friday night and hang out — once again — with my Christian friends. This new world of Churchland was sort of like a retreat into some sort of cozy Christian cocoon. We did good things for other people sometimes, like an annual trip to Mexico to build homes for needy families. A couple of times each year, we helped out at the local homeless shelter, serving meals and cleaning and painting the facility. We were also involved in getting help for local families each Christmas, providing meals and gifts for the parents to give to their children. But after we had finished these projects, we headed back to the suburbs to hang out with our Christian friends again. It happened so subtly, but the more I was immersed in Churchland, the more disconnected I felt from the world around me.

One signal that alerted me to the depth of my submersion in Churchland was when I found myself actually contemplating the purchase of a metallic Christian Fish for my 1966 Ford Mustang. Several of my friends had them on their Cavs, and at the time, it was the thing to do if you were a serious follower of Jesus. If you have no idea what I'm talking about, I'm referring to those chrome emblems you occasionally see on vehicles driven by Christians. These emblems are shaped like a fish because the symbol of the fish was used by the early Christians to identify those who followed Jesus. When Christians were persecuted by the Romans in the first centuries after Jesus, Christians used the symbol to mark their meeting places. One tradition tells how during times of persecution, when a Christian met a stranger in the road, the Christian drew one arc of the fish outline in the dirt. If the stranger drew the other arc, they knew that they both were Christians. The Greek word for fish, *ichthus*, was also an acronym for a slogan that confessed that Jesus Christ, God's Son, is Savior.

Now, there's nothing wrong with putting a fish on your car or on the cover of your Bible. But I remember wondering when I almost bought one because my friends had them, Why did I need to put this fish on my Mustang?

The fish symbol makes sense only to other Christians, people

who know what it means, and today it is more for decoration, since it doesn't have the same significance it did for Christians living during times of Roman persecution. I was once driving on the highway and saw a van that had two large fish emblems followed by two smaller fish emblems. I think it was trying to represent a mother, a father, and two kids in a cute, "Christian" way. But if I didn't already know what the fish symbol represents, I'd probably think, "That family is seriously into aquatic life." The fish doesn't communicate with outsiders who don't know the story behind the symbol.

What's amusing now is that after so many Christians put the fish symbol on their cars, someone created an alternative fish, the Darwin Fish, emblazoned with Charles Darwin's name and with tiny evolved legs growing out from under it.

Of course, defenders of the Christian fish couldn't allow this insult to go unchallenged, and they came back with the Christian counter-fish — the Truth Fish. In a not-so-subtle way, it suggests that the truth (the Bible and the Christian faith) is powerful enough to devour the alleged lies of the Darwin Fish.

*© Lana Sundman/Alamy*

While we may think this is cute or funny, it can make the church seem rather strange to those watching all of this from the outside. People who aren't part of Churchland watch Christians buy their metal fishes, Christian mints, Christian socks with Bible verses on them, and Christian poker chips with witty sayings on them (like "Jesus knows how to hold 'em" and "Don't gamble with eternity"). I'm sure the people who make these products are wonderfully good people with good intentions, but when we step back for a moment, we're forced to admit that it's all a bit odd. It's one of those strange things that happen whenever people hang out together for too long and lose perspective. Like the Pink Floyd song says, we become "comfortably numb" in the world of Churchland and lose our bearings, and we don't see how we can sometimes come across to people who are already suspicious of or confused about Christianity.

## BECOMING A CITIZEN OF CHURCHLAND

This might sound odd, but I believe that one of the biggest reasons there are so many negative perceptions of Christianity and the church is that Christians hang out with each other too much. Now, I know that as a Christian, I desperately need Christian friends in my life. They are a critical part of my healthy growth as a follower of Jesus. But what I learned as a new Christian entering the world of evangelical subculture is that there is a dark side to getting involved in too many Christian friendships. As we are immersed in these new friendships and our old activities are replaced with new, church-based activities, we slowly lose touch with our non-church-going friends. And the more we are involved in various forms of "Christian" activity, the less likely it is over time that we'll have friends who are not Christians (see chart).

I believe this is a major reason why for so many people the Christian faith ends up being defined by the extremes. Many of us have so few friendships with others outside the church that people see only the aggressive street evangelists or a pastor on the news who got caught in some scandal or who is being interviewed and saying some nutty things. If people don't see normal, day-to-day examples of real-life Christianity, then we shouldn't be surprised if the scandals and the extreme voices end up defining their view of the church.

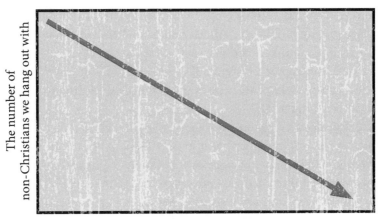

The longer we are Christians

The irony in all of this is that as we grow more mature, loving, and kind, learning what it means to follow Jesus, it becomes less likely that those outside the church will get to see and experience Jesus in us. We simply aren't around them in any significant way for them to notice.

Please don't misunderstand what I'm saying here. Christians absolutely do need to spend time with other Christians. But we should still seek to be *in* the world — though not *of* the world — just as Jesus taught us.[139] And we need to guard against becoming so focused on our involvement in Christian community that we don't spend enough time in the nonchurch community all around us.

When this happens to us, as it inevitably does, it's rarely intentional. We simply get more excited about the latest Christian concert or hearing some new music from a favorite Christian band than we do about engaging with people outside our church circles. We can't wait to travel to other countries to represent Jesus on summer missions trips. But when we return home from our adventures in distant lands, we aren't nearly as excited to represent Jesus to the people we work with every day, our neighbors, and our fellow students sitting next to us in class.

There are many subtle ways in which we can slowly become trapped in the world of Churchland. Some Christians might become fixated on certain minor theological beliefs and spend most of their time arguing with other Christians about detailed points of doctrine. Others might plunge into differing views of the apocalypse and become consumed by thoughts of the end times. They end up building relational fallout shelters with their Christian friends, bunkering down to wait for the end to come. For still others, the trap of Churchland might cause them to think that their specific views are always the right ones, leading to finger-pointing judgmentalism.

If you're a Christian, you may be thinking, "This isn't me at all." And I really hope that is true. But I'd still like to ask you to risk being uncomfortable for a moment. I'd like to invite you to evaluate yourself by asking some simple questions. How we spend our time and what we pray about are often representative of our hearts and our values. How would you answer the following questions?

- Who did you hang out with last weekend or the weekend before that? Or the weekend before that?
- When was the last time you spent time, in a social setting, with someone who doesn't attend your church?
- Who are you praying for regularly who is not a Christian?

These might sound like silly and overly simplistic questions to even have to ask, but how we spend our time and who we spend it with and what we pray about reveal a lot about us. Some of us might need to do some serious shifting in how we live our lives. If you desire to change the negative way so many people view the church and Christians, you need to show through your life that not all Christians are judgmental or negative or hateful or homophobic or whatever else people may think. People's perceptions won't change until they meet Christians who break the stereotypes.

In the end, it isn't really about defending or rebranding the church or Christianity; it's about following Jesus. It's about truly knowing Jesus and his life and teachings and, as a result, being changed into a new person. Christianity didn't change my life; Jesus did. But until I studied his teachings and learned what the Bible had to say, I really didn't know much about Jesus. I had a surface sort of understanding that was constantly clouded by my confusion over the church and Christianity.

But when I finally did study and learn about who Jesus is beneath the surface, everything changed. Everything.

# CHAPTER FOURTEEN

# BEYOND

★ ★ —OUR OWN— ★ ★

# PERSONAL JESUS

I'm not the King. Christ is the King. I'm just a singer.
— *Elvis Presley*

**I WAS WATCHING** an interview on television with a famous celebrity who was speaking about Jesus. I found it fascinating to listen to her, because she was speaking passionately about what Jesus would like, what he would do or say, and what he wouldn't like. She was telling everyone exactly what Jesus would support — politically, socially, and morally. But there was a problem. Her descriptions of Jesus weren't based on his actual teachings. Much of what she said about him even contradicted several of his teachings. It seemed to me as if she had caught a surface level understanding of Jesus, that he is a person of love and forgiveness (which he is!), but instead of looking more deeply into his life and his person, she had transferred her own understanding of those concepts onto Jesus.

This phenomenon isn't limited to celebrities. We sometimes do this in the church as well. A person with a strong sense of justice and caring for the poor likely will emphasize that part of

Jesus' teaching. Or a person who is into aggressive sports or wrestling may project those interests onto Jesus and prefer passages which speak of Jesus entering the battle with a sword. This is true of our temperaments as well. I am an introvert, so I often think of Jesus as being introverted. But if you are an extrovert, the life of the party, you are likely to envision Jesus as an extrovert. When you examine the wide variety of artistic depictions of Jesus, you'll find everything from a pale, passive, weak Jesus to a strong, muscular, WWF wrestler guy type of Jesus. We all too easily project our wishes and hopes onto Jesus, making him the Savior we want him to be.

There is a song by Depeche Mode called "Personal Jesus." It was inspired by how Priscilla Presley became so devoted to Elvis that he became Jesus-like to her. It's interesting how we can create our "own personal Jesus," making him who we want him to be, someone who looks like us. And this Jesus, of course, agrees with everything we believe. He likes the same music we do and likes the same churches we like. He agrees with our politics, liking what we like and disliking what we dislike. We all fall for this to some extent, whether we admit it or not. To avoid this danger, we need to return, again and again, to the Scriptures, the biblical accounts of Jesus' earliest followers, to learn who Jesus really is and to see if our beliefs align with what he teaches.

## MORE THAN A TEACHER OR A REVOLUTIONARY

It was both a joy and a challenge for me when I began to study and explore Jesus and his teachings on a deeper level. Underneath the confusion and messiness of church and Christianity, the most important question of all is, Who is Jesus? As I began to really dig down below the surface, I learned that the Bible doesn't present Jesus as just a good teacher. Though Jesus was a teacher who astonished people with his insight and his authoritative teaching, there is more to him than just his teaching.[140] Was Jesus a revolutionary? Yes, but there is more. Did Jesus' heart break with compassion for people?[141] Yes, but there is more. Did Jesus stand against religious legalism?[142] Yes, but there is more. All of these things are true about Jesus, but he is so much more than any one of these truths.

Volumes and volumes of books have been written about Jesus. As one of his own disciples wrote, "Jesus did many other things as well. If every one of them were written down, I suppose that even the whole world would not have room for the books that would be written."[143] As I read and studied the Bible, I realized that there was more to Jesus than I had thought. I'd heard bits and pieces of his story from television shows or references in songs. But I never understood that his story didn't begin in the town of Bethlehem when he was born.

It began in the beginning, in the first book of the Bible, the book of Genesis.

## IT DIDN'T BEGIN IN BETHLEHEM

In the book of Genesis, we read that God created human beings. We see that God was pleased with the people he made, saying that they were "very good."[144] The first human beings lived in what was called the garden of Eden, and God gave them freedom to do almost anything they wanted to do. He gave them the responsibility of caring for the earth and the creatures that he had made. It must have been beautiful, a time and place unlike any other. God also gave his first people free will, the ability to make their own decisions, but they chose not to listen to God, going against his guidance for their lives. By their own actions, they ended the innocence they had enjoyed, as well as the perfect harmony and beauty of their relationship with God, with each other, and with the creation itself. As a result, what we call sin entered the picture.[145] Sin is what happens when we choose to live in a way that is contrary to God's guidance for our lives.

Since God is loving and compassionate, caring for the people he had made, he didn't simply leave them alone to suffer the consequences of their actions. He didn't tell them, "Too bad. You blew it! You're on your own now." Instead, he provided for their needs and promised them that one day someone would come, one of their descendants, who would bring an end to the brokenness of the cursed world they now lived in. He would bring harmony to the disruption and discord they now faced because of their sin.[146] The story of the Hebrew Bible is the unfolding drama of God keeping this promise. We meet Abraham and learn that God has chosen to bless all the people on earth through one of his descendants.[147] We see the promise continued in King David, that this descendant would also be a king who would rule over God's creation with justice.[148] Prophets from Israel prophesied about who this future person would be, including specific prophecies about his super-natural birth, that he would be born of a virgin.[149]

As you can see, though we often think of Jesus' story beginning with his birth, the virgin birth is really the fulfillment of a prom-ise, the next chapter in an even larger story that began way back in the beginning with creation. The Christmas story tells us of Jesus' miraculous birth to a girl named Mary, who was a virgin.[150] When I first heard about a virgin giving birth, it did sound fairly crazy to me, but I tried to remain open-minded. I reasoned that if Jesus was a unique person who would fulfill all of God's promises to us, then God would want to make his birth distinct in some way. And after reading in the Bible about other miracles that God has done, this one didn't seem all that improbable. God, as he is presented in the Bible, seems able to do whatever he wants. If he can create the universe, then having a virgin give birth doesn't seem all that unusual for him.

What stunned me, even more than the fact of the virgin birth, was realizing that Jesus' birth and so many of the events of his life had been predicted long beforehand. Prophets who had lived hun-dreds of years before wrote down predictions in the Hebrew Bible with specific details about his birth, life, and death. They predicted he would be born of a virgin, that he would be from the lineage of King David, and that his kingship and rule would be greater in some way than a typical king.[151] It was prophesied that Jesus would have his ministry in the Galilee area (in modern-day Israel)[152] and that he would teach people using parables.[153] I learned it was fore-told that Jesus would care about the poor and the marginalized.[154] Incredibly, the Hebrew Bible also prophesied that Jesus' teachings would stir up trouble and that he would be rejected, betrayed, and even killed for what he taught.[155] The Hebrew Scriptures include a poetic description of the type of death he would die — on a cross — long before crucifixions were invented.[156]

The Bible also teaches that Jesus had emotions, and he wept, and he got tired. He ate and drank wine and was fully human in every way.[157] Classical artwork sometimes portrays Jesus with a glowing halo, making him seem superhuman, but that's not how he appeared when he lived. He looked like an ordinary person. But there was something wonderful about Jesus as well. Though he was fully human, just as we are, and could relate to our pain, our struggles, and our temptations, the Scriptures also teach us that Jesus was God, fully divine. As one theologian explains, "In the person of Jesus, God physically entered into our world. An infinite God came to live in a finite world. The one who knew exactly how things were supposed to be came to a place where things obviously weren't. In Jesus, God and man became one person. Jesus Christ was, and forever will be, fully God and fully man in one person. And that one person changed the course of history forever."[158]

I understand that the idea that Jesus is God sounds bizarre and very different from the Jesus we may generally think of. And it sounds that way because it *is* bizarre and different. This is not a normal story. It is the story of God intervening in history, acting out of his love for people. I remember when I first encountered all of this, I thought, "Yikes! I had no idea the Bible ever said that." But the longer I studied and the more I thought about it, the more beautiful and wonderful it became to me. I remember coming across a story told by the evangelist Billy Graham that was quite helpful to me at the time. Talking about Jesus and why God became man, Graham said, "You know one day I was walking along and I stepped on an anthill. And I thought to myself as I saw those dying ants, I wish I could go down and be an ant for just a moment to talk to those ants and tell them that I didn't mean to. That's the way it was with God. God looked down over the battlements of heaven and God said, 'How can I tell men that I'm a God of love, I'm a God of mercy, that I'm a God of longsuffering; the only way I can do it is to become a man.' And that's exactly what happened, ladies and gentlemen: Jesus Christ became man."[159]

## THE MEANING OF "A SAVIOR IS BORN" ON A CHRISTMAS CARD

The more I read and studied what the Bible says about who Jesus is, the more the intensity of my wonder about him grew. The Jesus I was discovering in the Bible was both eye-opening and heart-opening. I remember when I finally understood what the phrase "a

Savior is born" actually means.[160] I'd seen the words on Christmas cards, usually floating in the night sky above the manger scene, but I didn't really know what it means that Jesus is a savior.

As I was studying, it became clear that the Bible teaches that when our thoughts or actions don't follow God's guidance and instruction, it is considered sin. Sin is another word I hadn't understood. Translated from the Greek, it means "to miss the mark" of God's holy guidance for our lives. So sin is when we choose to think we are smarter than God (whether or not we realize that's what we're doing) and act on what we think is best for ourselves rather than follow God's guidance. As I reflected on this and read more, I began to really grieve about a lot of the things I had done in my life, times when I hurt people, when I lied, when I was selfish at someone else's expense — I could go on and on.

Until I read Scripture, I never really had a standard to compare my life and actions with. Though I knew I wasn't perfect, I didn't think I was that bad of a person, but all of a sudden I started developing a sense of remorse. It's like when you don't notice how dirty your laptop screen is until sunlight or a bright light hits it, and then you notice everything. That's what happened to me as I read the Bible. I wish I could put it into words. It wasn't just guilt, like I got caught stealing candy. It was like I hurt a friend or let someone down, and this friend was God.[161]

As I was trying to process all of this, I was greatly relieved to read that the Bible says that everyone has sinned.[162] So I wasn't alone. But then I wondered, How do I get forgiven for all of the messes I made in my life? And I realized it was through Jesus. I read the parts of the Bible that say that Jesus is the mediator between us and God.[163] Jesus went to the cross, and it was by his death there that our sins are forgiven. Out of love, Jesus paid the cost of all of our actions against God and his guidance.[164]

I didn't understand it all. So many questions came up. Why death on a cross? I didn't like reading that Jesus had to die, especially for me. But the more I read, the more I understood that it happened because this thing called sin is so messy and ugly; I understood that Jesus saved us from having to pay the consequences of our selfishness and of all of the pain we have caused others. Deep inside, I realized that I did need a savior. And suddenly those nice words on a Christmas card became the most important reality in my life. Jesus is my Savior, and I put my faith in him. I didn't understand it all, but I believed.

I look back now years after those early days when I was learning about Jesus, and I am still amazed, overjoyed, and thankful beyond any words I could express. The Bible taught me that all we've ever done in our lives that falls short of what God intended when he made us is covered by what Jesus did on the cross. Our wrongs and our selfish rejection of God's ways are one hundred percent forgiven.

But that's not the end of the story.

## A DEAD MAN ON A STICK

I was in a supermarket a few Easter seasons ago, and in front of me were a father and daughter waiting in line. There was a religious card in the aisle with a piece of art on it depicting Jesus on the cross. The daughter, a young girl around five or six years old, pointed to the crucifix and asked her dad, "What is that?" The dad looked at the card and said to his daughter, "Oh, that's just a dead man on a stick." Obviously, it wasn't the right place to start a discussion with him, but I have to admit that I badly wanted to say, "No! The story doesn't end with Jesus on the cross. He arose from the grave!"

I will never forget that sense of amazement I felt when I read for the first time how Jesus physically resurrected from the dead.[165] Though it might sound crazy to talk about someone coming back to life after being dead for several days, this reality lies at the heart of the Christian faith. Though the cross is what secures our forgiveness for the mess we've made of our lives and of the world, it is Jesus' resurrection that offers us hope. Because Jesus conquered the power of death, we no longer need to fear our own deaths.[166] The resurrection demonstrates that everything Jesus said is true, and shows us that he is unique among all the people who have ever lived. The Bible teaches us that when Jesus returns, he will restore God's ways and make everything new again.[167] When we talk about Jesus and what he did, we're talking about something unprecedented and miraculous.

I know that for some, this all sounds quite crazy. Recently I was talking to someone who is not a Christian, and he was asking me some questions about Jesus. At one point, he asked me, very sincerely, if I thought Jesus was a zombie. It was a little humorous to hear him ask that, but I could understand his perspective. Zombies are people who die and then come back to life. And zombies are everywhere today in movies and computer games. So when someone hears the story of the resurrection for the first time — that Jesus died and came back to life — it makes total sense that they might relate it to the idea of being a zombie.

The truth about Jesus can be hard to believe. It's quite strange and unusual. But let's not forget that it was strange and unusual in Jesus' day as well. At the heart of what Jesus taught his followers is an astounding truth about his death and resurrection from the dead. Jesus himself spoke to his disciples for several weeks after his death and resurrection, appearing to hundreds of people. In one of the earliest records we have of the message they shared with people (the gospel or "good news"), Paul the apostle wrote, "For what I received I passed on to you as of first importance: that Christ died for our sins according to the Scriptures, that he was buried, that he was raised on the third day according to the Scriptures, and that he appeared to Cephas, and then to the Twelve. After that, he appeared to more than five hundred of the brothers and sisters at the same time, most of whom are still living, though some have fallen asleep. Then he appeared to James, then to all the apostles, and last of all he appeared to me also, as to one abnormally born."[168]

The followers of Jesus really believed that Jesus was who he said he was, and they claimed to have seen him and talked with him for several weeks after he was raised from the dead. Their lives were so changed by Jesus that they were even willing to die for what they believed when they were persecuted for their faith. If the disciples hadn't really seen the risen Jesus and it was some sort of hoax or fable, there's no way they would have been willing to suffer and even be killed for something they knew wasn't true.

## MORE THAN SAYING A PRAYER AND WAITING FOR HEAVEN

After Jesus resurrected from the dead, he gave his followers a mission: telling others about what he had done and teaching others the way of life that he had taught them.[169] This is an important part of the story, one that we often forget. The church was born for this very mission. Jesus didn't just call his followers to believe in him as their Savior; he sent them out to follow him and serve the world on his mission. Jesus didn't tell his followers to sit around, attending church meetings and singing songs, just waiting to die and then go to be with him in heaven. Instead, Jesus told his followers to go into the world and with the power of God's Spirit live as people on a mission from God, bringing the love and the message of Jesus to others.[170] And his disciples did just that. The church was created not to be an inwardly focused group of passive people but a church with an outward focus, on a mission to serve others in the world.[171]

The Bible teaches us that Jesus is still involved in the world today, through the presence of God's Spirit and the work of the church, made up of his followers. According to the Bible, after several weeks of teaching his disciples, Jesus ascended into heaven and promised them that one day he would return to this world — in flesh and blood — to call us all, both living and dead, to account for our lives.[172] Jesus' story is more than just the tale of his life as a carpenter and a Jewish rabbi. It is the story line of the entire Bible, a narrative that begins in the beginning of time and gives us a glimpse of a future that has yet to unfold. It's bigger than I could possibly have ever imagined.

## NO ORDINARY STORY

Jesus' story is not an ordinary story. It sets Jesus apart from other religious leaders in significant ways. There's so much more that we come to learn about Jesus when we read the entire account of him in the Bible. The main reason I write books like this and share my stories is because I really believe that Jesus has the power to change lives. Reading about him isn't like reading the story of Thomas Edison or Abraham Lincoln or Martin Luther King Jr. Reading about these men has changed me in various ways, since they all are inspiring historical figures, but Jesus got into my heart, mind, and soul in a way that other historical figures did not.

Some who are reading this chapter know Jesus already. My hope for those who don't know much about Jesus is that you will take some time to consider him. I'm not trying to sell you something, like those late-night infomercials for a mop or a set of knives that promise, "If you buy this, your life will be changed!" We all know when we see these ads that the hype is bigger than the truth. But Jesus isn't a late-night product, even though some have tried to sell him as one; he's very much the real thing. People all over the world and down through history have freely confessed that trusting Jesus and believing his message has changed their lives. And that's my story as well. If you knew me before I put faith in Jesus, you would know I am a changed person. One of my many tendencies was to be critical and selfish, caring much more about myself than about others. I know I can still tend to be this way, but I also know that God has helped me to change and still is helping me to change.

I share all of this because some of you likely have never put your faith in Jesus. You may have some very understandable concerns and doubts about the miraculous and supernatural aspects of Jesus and the teachings of the Bible, or you may not like what you've seen of Christianity and the church. Believe me, I understand, because I had doubts and concerns too. I had so many questions. There were plenty of things I didn't like about the church. But once I looked past the messiness of Christianity and the church and instead focused on learning about Jesus, something changed. Actually, that's an understatement — everything changed. Jesus was no longer just "Jesus." He became my Savior.

## THE "KING" SAYS JESUS IS KING

I've long been a fan of the music of Elvis Presley. I don't know exactly what Elvis believed about Jesus. His stepbrother claims that Elvis was a Christian, but we also know that there were long periods in his life when he clearly was not walking with God. Still, those close to Elvis have said that despite his frequent wanderings from the faith, he always came back to his belief in Jesus. Apparently, even on the night of his death, Elvis prayed for forgiveness, saying that he wanted to live for Jesus.

Regardless of what Elvis did or didn't do in his desire to follow Jesus, there is a wonderful story that I once heard about a woman who saw him at a concert in Las Vegas. She approached Elvis with a large sign that boldly stated that he was the King. Much to her surprise, Elvis responded by correcting her.

"No, honey, I'm not the King," he said. "Christ is the King. I'm just a singer."

I've always really liked that quote, especially coming from Elvis. There are so many things we can say about Jesus. There has never been anyone like Jesus, no one who has had the same effect on history or who has changed as many lives. Elvis was right saying Jesus is King. He is the King of Kings and the Lord of Lords, as the Bible describes him.[173] That's the amazing thing I discovered about Jesus many years ago, even in the often confusing messiness of Christianity and the church.

And my life has never been the same.

# CHAPTER FIFTEEN

# JOHNNY CASH
## ★ ★ ── AND ── ★ ★
# JESUS

Now pay close attention ... it's somebody you oughta know
You know it's all about a man that walked on earth nearly
    two thousand years ago ...
Who was it everybody? (It was Jesus) It was Jesus Christ our
    Lord

*—Johnny Cash, "It Was Jesus"*

## BELIEF BEYOND BOBBLE-HEADS AND ACTION FIGURES

I am pretty sure I would have given up on the church long ago if it weren't for Jesus. Through all my struggles with the church and my questions about the Christian faith, it was Jesus who kept moving in my heart and mind and kept me interested in learning more. It was Jesus who won me over, and it was his vision for the church that kept me from leaving the church to follow God on my own. The more time I spent studying about Jesus, the more I saw that there was more to him than just his teachings and a philosophy of life. Time after time, in the stories of the Bible, Jesus spoke about believing in him. He talked about trusting him, and how with that trust comes forgiveness of sin and eternal life. Jesus did more than model a compassionate way to live. He once said to a woman who had just lost her brother, "I am the resurrection and the life. The one who believes in me will live, even though they die; and whoever lives by believing in me will never die."[174]

I couldn't ignore these words. Eventually at some point during the time I was trying to make sense of Christianity, I believed. I didn't put my faith in Christianity; I put my faith in Jesus. I can't even say exactly when it happened, but sometime during my questioning and studying, I believed that Jesus is who he said he is. I didn't have a big, memorable conversion experience. There were no flashing lights or choirs of angels appearing in the sky. While some people have dramatic experiences when they first come to trust Jesus, for me it happened more gradually, over time. It was more like slowly getting to know someone, like an acquaintance you meet one day and start hanging out with occasionally. At first, I read my Bible and studied. Then, I started praying to God. I began to sense that God was with me all the time and that he cared about me. My times of prayer and reading the Bible became more frequent. My prayers became more conversational. Before I knew what was happening, God was a regular part of my life. One day, it was as though we were good friends.

That's how I began to walk with Jesus. And though I wasn't fully aware of it at the time, I believe that God was very much involved in all of that, drawing me toward him, something I probably never would have done on my own.[175] So the simple explanation for why I became a Christian is that God drew me to him.[176] I had no bottoming-out experience. I had no one pressuring me. I just little by little learned who Jesus is and then slowly began to trust him.

It was pretty freaky for me when I did put my faith in Jesus and become a Christian. I was really encouraged and comforted to learn I wasn't alone in this experience. Intelligent people I admired, like professors and authors C. S. Lewis and J. R. R. Tolkien, were Christians and trusted in Jesus. There are doctors, scientists, professors, lawyers, and other intelligent people who put faith in Jesus. Even some of my rockabilly heroes, like Carl Perkins (who wrote "Blue Suede Shoes") and Sun Studio drummer Jimmy

Van Eaton (who drummed on many of Jerry Lee Lewis's big hits) were Christians. Jonny Ray Bartel, who was in a well-known blues band called the Red Devils and is now in one of my favorite punk-rockabilly bands, the Knitters, turned out to be a Christian, and he is now a good friend. In those early days of following Jesus and not resonating with the popular evangelical Christian music of that time, I discovered a "Christian" band called the Altar Boys who played the punkish type of music I liked.[177] It was a huge relief to me as a punk and rockabilly musician to know that others of my musical kind out there were also Christians.

## THE MAN IN BLACK WHO BELIEVED IN JESUS

One musician in particular was instrumental in helping me choose to follow Christ and grow as a Christian. His name was Johnny Cash, and he was one of the Sun Studio originals. Our band used to play a punk-hillbilly version of his hit song "I Walk the Line." It seemed as if everyone, regardless of whether they liked rockabilly or country, appreciated Johnny Cash and his music. He was widely admired, and since I loved rockabilly music, Johnny Cash was at the dead center of my circle of admiration.

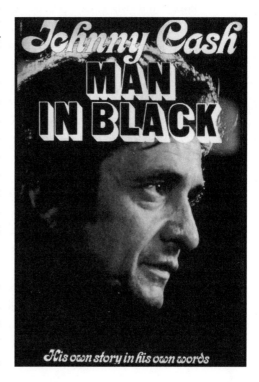

As I was still growing in my faith, I stumbled upon a book written by Johnny Cash, an autobiography titled *Man in Black* that was published way back in 1975. In this book, Cash was honest about his long-term battle with drug addiction and about the darker seasons in his life. But the surprising conclusion to the story was that he had eventually put his faith in Jesus. Though there were ongoing struggles, Johnny Cash's faith in Jesus remained constant over the years, helping him to overcome his addictions. I learned that Johnny Cash was a regular church attender, involved in Hendersonville Baptist Church near his home. After the *Man in Black* book, Cash wrote another book about Paul the apostle called *The Man in White*. I also read that he had even travelled to Israel to film a movie about Jesus' life, paying for it out of his own pocket. He had also done an audio recording of the entire Bible, as well as played music at several Christian events. He had even recorded several gospel music albums and remained solid in his Christian faith for his whole life.

I was totally shocked to learn that Johnny Cash was a Christian. After all, he was the coolest of cool, the man in black. It was so wild discovering the book that he wrote about it. And it was his honesty that drew me into reading his story. Cash was open about his struggles, and the ups and downs of his life seemed authentic. He hadn't just disappeared into the Christian subculture. As I followed Johnny Cash's life over the years since then, I appreciated a description he once gave of different types of Christians: "There's preaching Christians, church-playing Christians, and there's practicing Christians. I'm trying to be a practicing Christian. If you take the words of Jesus literally and apply them in everyday life, you discover that the greatest fulfillment you'll ever find really is giving. And that's why I do things like prison concerts. Compared to that, projects like the television I did, for example, have very little meaning for me."[178]

Johnny Cash challenged the church to be faithful to the Bible, to be more than just a self-focused community. He believed that the call to follow Jesus is a call to serve others: "To go into church is great, but to go out and put it all into action, that's where it all is at."[179]

Even though he was a popular music star and a public figure, Johnny Cash was quite bold in telling others he was a Christian, but he tried to do it in a way that would get people to think. Once, when he appeared on television to perform, he said, "I'm not here tonight to exalt Johnny Cash. I'm standing here as an entertainer, as a performer, as a singer who is supporting the gospel of Jesus Christ. I'm here to invite you to listen to the good news that will be laid out for you, to analyze it, and see if you don't think it's the best way to live." He wasn't forceful in presenting his faith, but he never hid what he believed or who he was.

I know that my faith rests on Jesus alone, but I do have to admit that when I heard Johnny Cash was such a devout Christian, I was greatly encouraged. Because he was someone I highly admired and was also a musician, it didn't feel as crazy that I was a Christian. Reading about how Johnny was public about his faith also helped me to see that I too didn't have to be embarrassed to let others know that I was a Christian. And seeing that Cash was committed to and deeply involved in his church helped me to believe that belonging to a church was possible for me. I figured that if someone like Johnny Cash could be a Christian and attend a church, Christianity can't be all that bad.

## WANDA JACKSON, THE QUEEN OF ROCKABILLY

After I learned that Johnny Cash was a Christian, it was very cool to learn that Wanda Jackson, another of my rockabilly heroes, also followed Jesus. For those who don't know her, Wanda Jackson recently was inducted into the Rock and Roll Hall of Fame and is widely respected as a pioneer in the music world. She was one of the very first women to enter the rockabilly scene back in the mid-1950s, and she even dated Elvis Presley for a while. It was through Elvis that she began singing, touring with Elvis, Johnny Cash, Jerry Lee Lewis, and many of the popular rock and roll musicians of that time. She is spoken highly of and admired by artists like Bruce Springsteen, Elvis Costello, Adele (whom she has toured with), and many other respected musicians. Wanda has even been dubbed the Queen of Rockabilly.[180] But not only is Wanda a rockabilly legend, she and her husband, Wendell, are passionate followers of Jesus.

I've had the joy of hanging out with Wanda and Wendell several times and have personally heard the story of how they came to know and follow Jesus. Jesus changed their lives, and Wanda can't help but want to tell others about him. She does this in a very respectful yet bold way. Every single time that she performs, she takes some time in the middle of the concert to stop playing, quieting everyone down. Then, for about two minutes, she shares with them her faith in Jesus, talking about how he has changed her life. She is careful to let the crowd know that she is aware that they didn't come to the concert to hear about Jesus, and is almost apologetic out of respect for her fans. But in a humble yet winsome way, Wanda shares her faith with those who are willing to listen, telling them why Jesus means so much to her.

Recently, I was backstage at a show with Wanda and Wendell, and they told me how they value the opportunity they have to be a "witness" for Jesus. (That was the word they used.) Wanda recognizes that God has given her a prominent place in the music world, and the way she shares her faith fits who she is and how God has made her. Everywhere she goes, Wanda lets others know that she is a Christian. And every time she shares that, it breaks down the stereotypes that people have of Christians, helping people see that following Jesus isn't what they may have thought.

## BREAKING STEREOTYPES ABOUT CHRISTIANS AND THE CHURCH

Johnny Cash, Wanda Jackson, C. S. Lewis, J. R. R. Tolkien, and many others like them give me hope. Hope that we can change the negative impressions that people have of Christianity and the church. People may still disagree with what Christians believe, but when followers of Jesus truly represent him to the world, it shows them that not all Christians are judgmental, anti-gay, anti-science, chauvinistic, biblical literalists. Nor is the church just an organized religion that tries to control or stifle people.

Jesus taught his followers not to stay all together and remain in the church building but to be "in the world."[181] While clearly warning his followers not to participate in evil, he also prayed that they would be his loving witnesses to those who didn't know God: "My prayer is not that you take them out of the world.... As you sent me into the world, I have sent them into the world."[182] Christians are called to winsomly, lovingly, humbly represent Jesus, sharing what Jesus has said and done and modeling that in their lives and relationships with others. If Jesus' followers aren't in the world, instead choosing to spend most of their time with other Christians, then we aren't functioning as Jesus' church. And we lose the opportunity to break some of the negative stereotypes about the church and Christianity.

As you have learned through my own story, it is real people just doing their best to follow Jesus who end up making the biggest impact on the world. I know that I never would have had any interest in the church:

- if I hadn't met some Christians who broke my stereotypes.
- if I hadn't found a church that welcomed me.
- if I hadn't begun reading what the Bible says about following Jesus.
- if I hadn't understood who Jesus really is.
- if I hadn't understood that Jesus loves people — messed-up, broken people — and calls them to learn what it means to follow him together, representing him in mission to the world by loving one another and the people around them just as he would.

I was talking to a pastor once about the need for Christians to avoid clustering in their own subculture and the importance of being out in the world, dispelling the stereotypes and negative impressions that people have about Christianity. He joked that perhaps it would be best if some Christians actually stayed where they were, hidden from sight. That could be true for some. But not all who follow Jesus are crazy. Most are just normal people, doing their best to follow Jesus, despite their mistakes and failures. All I ask is that you consider that what you sometimes see isn't the church the way Jesus intended it to be.

But if that is true, it raises an entirely different question for us to consider. What is the church, according to Jesus?

And would Jesus, if he were still living on earth today, even attend one of our churches? That's a question worth exploring.

# CHAPTER SIXTEEN

Christ loved the church and gave himself up for her.
— *Ephesians 5:25*

**WHEN PEOPLE THINK** of the church, they often reflect on their experience attending a service on a Sunday morning. They think of visiting a building and seeing people wearing robes sitting in a choir. Or they think of a stage with a pulpit and a preacher. Or they think of the worship band with flashing lights and everyone singing in a darkened room together. I've found it quite important to clarify what we mean when we talk about the church by defining the term and explaining what the Bible teaches. Only after we understand what the church is can we answer the question, Would Jesus go to a church?

## WHAT IS *CHURCH*?

The word *church* was not some new word that the writers of the Bible made up. It was a word commonly used in Jesus' day. In Greek, which is the language in which the New Testament was written, it is the word *ekklesia*, which means "an assembly" or "a gathering." It is derived from the verb *ekkaleo*, a compound of *ek* ("out") and *kaleo* ("to call"), which together means "to call out."[183] Before Jesus and his followers began using this word, it most commonly referred to the nonreligious gathering of people for political purposes, meetings in which citizens made decisions regarding laws, office appointments, and public policy.[184] *Ekklesia* did not refer to a building or a location; it referred to the people as they assembled together.

If we were to translate the word *ekklesia* into English today, we could just as easily use the word *gathering* or *assembly* instead of the word *church*. Unfortunately, when the word *ekklesia* was first translated into the English language, a word with a slightly different meaning was used, causing lasting confusion about the true sense of the word. Our English word *church* is not directly related to the word *ekklesia* in the sense of a gathering or meeting. Instead, *church* comes from yet another Greek word, one that was used after the writing of the New Testament to describe Christian houses of worship — the Greek word *kuriakon*. This word, from which we get the Scottish word *kirk*, the German word *kirche*, and the Old English word *cirice*, means "belonging to the Lord." It was used to refer to the Lord's "house," the building where Christians regularly gathered for worship.

Now, you might be wondering, Why does any of this matter? It matters because over time, the word that we find in the New Testament used to describe the people of God called out by God to engage in God's mission (*ekklesia*) became replaced by a word that referred to a building — the church.

In 1526, a man named William Tyndale noticed growing corruption in the church. Among the many problems he identified was this mistranslation of the word *ekklesia*. The common assumption in his day was that the church was a building, as well as an institution of great power and authority, distinct from the common people. So Tyndale decided to translate *ekklesia* as *congregation*, indicating that the church is the gathered people of God, not a building or an institution. This infuriated the church leaders of his day, who wanted to retain their power and authority, their control of the institutional church. They feared what would happen if the Bible made its way into the hands of common people, so they had William Tyndale burned at the stake. Tyndale was a martyr for his faith, someone who gave his life to help people understand biblical teaching about the church. He wanted people to know that the church they knew — the church seen as a building and an institution controlled by corrupt leaders — was not the church that Jesus envisioned.

## TECHNICALLY, IT'S IMPOSSIBLE TO "GO TO CHURCH"

Despite Tyndale's efforts, we continue to make the same mistake today. The truth is that none of us can really "go" to church. If the church is people, then it's a theological, not to mention logical, impossibility for us to go to church. Think of it this way. My last name is Kimball. I can't *go* to Kimball, because I *am* Kimball. In fact, there is not a single Bible verse that tells us to "go to church," because the writers of the New Testament and the earliest Christians didn't think of the church this way. If you were to travel back in time to the days of the early church and ask a Christian, "Are you going to church this Sunday?" he would probably give you a blank stare.

Unfortunately, we constantly reinforce this erroneous understanding of the church as a place that we go to. We so often hear phrases like:

"Welcome to church!"
"Are you going to church?"
"Let's go to church this Sunday."
"I'm going to attend church this week."

In addition to the problem of mistranslating the Greek word *ekklesia*, some of the confusion comes from a failure to understand the unfolding story line of the Bible. You see, prior to the destruction of the temple in Jerusalem in AD 70, the place where God dwelled with his people was most commonly thought of as a particular place — a building (the temple) or a tent (the tabernacle). Both of these places were even called "God's house,"[185] and this understanding of God's house as a place where people could meet with God is found throughout the Old Testament. But with the coming of Jesus and in the teaching of the early church, we see a significant shift. The followers of Jesus, even before the destruction of the temple, taught that the house of God was no longer a temple or a building;

it was the gathering of God's people. With the coming of Jesus and the giving of the gift of God's Spirit to his followers, God no longer dwells in a building; the Spirit of God dwells in people.[186] This is why the Bible teaches that the bodies of Christians are the temple of God's Spirit and that God dwells in the midst of his gathered people. This means that God's house is not a church building; it's people. You don't enter some special magical building called "God's house," where God is inside that space more than outside it. God's house is now in the people of God wherever they are, whether it's in the parking lot, in a bowling alley, or in an office cubicle.

## A NURSERY RHYME FROM THE DEVIL

I often joke that I've traced the continuation of this misunderstanding about the church to an evil nursery rhyme. Obviously, I'm kidding, but I am concerned about a rhyme that many Christians teach their kids. It's a cute little saying, but it perpetuates a significant misunderstanding of what the church is. Children, from a young age, are taught to put their fingers into the shape of a church steeple and say, "Here is the church, here is the steeple, open the doors and see all the people."

But the rhyme is a hundred percent wrong.

Whenever we recite this rhyme with our children, we teach them that the church is something other than the people. Here is the church (meaning the building). And there, when you look inside the church building, are the people. This leads our children to think of church as a place they go to, and it can become just another place for them. Instead, I suggest an alternate version of the rhyme, one that emphasizes the biblical understanding of the church as the called out people of God: "Here is the church made up of people, sitting in a building that has a pretty steeple."

I have sometimes wondered if one of my callings in life is to find every Sunday school curriculum in the world and replace the words of this rhyme with a theologically correct version.

## DON'T GO TO CHURCH TODAY

My point in sharing this isn't simply to correct trivial vocabulary. I believe that the way we use this word subtly affects how we think.

Instead of saying, "I am going to church," I say to people, "I'm going to the church gathering," or, "I'm going to where the church meets." In our church, we no longer refer to our meetings on Sunday mornings as church services (a phrase which reminds me of receiving service at a gas station and then leaving). Instead, we say that we have Sunday gatherings, where the church gathers for worship and teaching. Our language is an expression of our theology, so it matters that our words are as true to the Bible as possible.

For some people, it's a huge shift to think of church as something other than a place where they go or an event that takes place on a Sunday. But when we understand that we are called to *be* the church, not just go to church, it changes our identity. No longer do we go to a building where religious activities happen and that is "church." We now are the church all week long. This affects our sense of mission and purpose as well. Jesus told his followers to be in the world, not to hide from it.[187] The church is people who represent Jesus to the world. The Bible even refers to followers of Jesus as his "ambassadors,"[188] people called to represent the country they are from (the kingdom of heaven) and the leader or king they serve (King Jesus).

As God's ambassadors, when we speak and act, we represent Jesus' words and actions. The church should care about the things Jesus cares about and do the things that Jesus would do. But an ambassador doesn't just represent someone by their presence; they speak on behalf of the one they represent. The church speaks on Jesus' behalf, telling the world the wonderful news about his life, death, and resurrection and how he has made a way for people to be reconciled to God. The church represents Jesus by caring for those in need, the marginalized and oppressed, just as Jesus would care for them.

As Christians, being the church means we represent Jesus every day of the week to all sorts of people: to our families, our spouses, the people we work with, our neighbors, the waitress in the restaurant, the clerk at the supermarket, the receptionist at the doctor's office, the person who issues parking tickets, people who like a different style of music than you do, people who have opinions about theology that differ from yours, the parent with the crying baby on the plane, and the restless teenager in the youth group. We represent Jesus to the single, married, divorced, widowed, straight, gay, lesbian, bisexual, and transgendered. We represent Jesus to the Buddhist, the Hindu, the Muslim, the atheist, and the agnostic. We represent Jesus to the rich, the poor, the middle class, to the person who steals from us, and to the person who gives something to us.

When we think of church primarily as a place or an event we go to, we minimize the theologically rich identity of the church as the people of God. And this identity — of *being* the church — is more than a passive statement about who we are; it's also a call to action. As representatives of Jesus, those called to communicate and live out his message and the message about him, we are on a mission.

| The Church Isn't | The Church Is |
|---|---|
| A building that Christians meet in | Followers of Jesus, wherever they are throughout the week |
| A service you go to on Sunday (it's a theological impossibility to "go to church") | A community that gathers on Sunday to worship and serve God |
| A Sunday meeting where religious professionals give sermons and lead people in singing songs while they sit in rows and watch | A missional community that meets on various days of the week whose pastors and leaders train, support, and help the church understand their giftedness and how God made them to participate in Jesus' mission |
| Successful if decisions for Jesus are made | Successful if disciples of Jesus are made |
| A place you go to be a consumer, like in a shopping mall | A community that cares for each other as they serve the world |
| A community whose mission is to alert people to wrongs in culture and to judge the world | A community whose mission is to alert people to the universal reign of God through Jesus by proclamation and demonstration |
| Go to church | *Be* the church |

## THE CHURCH IS NOT ABOUT SERVING US; IT'S ABOUT SERVING OTHERS

When we look at what Jesus said to his twelve disciples when he first called them and what he said to them years later the last day he was on earth, it's interesting that both times he emphasized their unique mission. When he called his disciples, he said, "Come, follow me ... and I will send you out to fish for people."[189] Jesus was speaking to vocational fishermen, so he used the fishing metaphor to communicate a new purpose for their lives. Unlike the fishing they were used to doing, this new type of fishing involved being sent out into the world to find other people and share with them the joy, life, and peace that come from knowing Jesus. They would now be fishing for people.

Notice that Jesus doesn't say to them, "Come, follow me, and I will send you into buildings to retreat from the world, protect yourselves from evil, and create your own Christian subculture." Jesus didn't say, "Come, follow me, and I will send you once a week into a church building where paid religious professionals lead you in singing some songs, preach a sermon to you, and then send you home to go about your own business for the rest of the week." Jesus didn't say, "Come, follow me, and I will turn you into a judgmental, inwardly focused people." He called his followers to lovingly share his message and represent him to the world. From the very beginning, when Jesus called people to follow him, he called them to focus on others. Jesus told his disciples that following him was not just about living for themselves; it was about serving others.[190]

Not only were Jesus' first recorded words about mission, but we also find that his last recorded words were about mission as well. According to the gospel of Matthew, after Jesus resurrected and prior to his ascension to heaven, his last words to his disciples were, "Go and make disciples of all nations, baptizing them in the name of the Father and of the Son and of the Holy Spirit, and teaching them to obey everything I have commanded you. And surely I am with you always, to the very end of the age."[191] Jesus didn't send his followers to settle down comfortably in Churchland; he wanted them to be outwardly focused, going out into the world, not just to make converts or have people make quick decisions, but to make disciples. Disciples are those who model themselves after another person, like an apprentice does. This means building relationships, teaching, and commiting to adjust life to the teachings of Jesus.

## THE CHURCH DOESN'T SERVE ALONE

Being on mission isn't always easy, but notice that Jesus also promises to be with his followers. In yet another account of Jesus' last words from the book of Acts, we see Jesus reinforcing the call to be outwardly focused while promising his followers that they will be uniquely equipped with power to accomplish their mission. Jesus says to them, "It is not for you to know the times or dates the Father has set by his own authority. But you will receive power when the Holy Spirit comes on you; and you will be my witnesses in Jerusalem, and in all Judea and Samaria, and to the ends of the earth."[192] Jesus told his disciples that instead of trying to figure out the when and where of the end times, they should instead be out in the world, sharing God's love with people. And Jesus encouraged his followers by reminding them that they weren't alone in this calling, that God would give them the gift of the Holy Spirit.

When Jesus called people to follow him, he made it clear that they would not need to rely simply upon human effort and ability. Jesus promised his followers that God would send his Spirit to empower, strengthen, and guide them in their work.[193] This is what makes the church a unique community. It is a supernatural community empowered by God for a mission. The work that the church does is not just about developing programs, providing good inspirational messages, and offering excellent children's ministry. Nor is it simply about caring for the poor or working to bring justice to those who are oppressed. The church is called to do all of these things, but not alone, relying on mere human wisdom and strength. The mission of the church is a mission given by God, and the church fulfills its mission when it relies upon God's Spirit to accomplish God's work on earth.[194]

## ON MISSION FROM THE START

As the story unfolds, God's Spirit does indeed come, empowering Jesus' disciples in a dramatic way. The church is born.[195] It's fascinating to notice that the first thing the church does after receiving the gift of God's Spirit is to share the good news about Jesus with other people.[196] The very first thing! From the moment of its birth, the church existed to share the story about the work and teaching of Jesus, why he came and what he did to change the world forever. The message that the early church shared was all about Jesus: his life, his death, and his resurrection.[197] Jesus' earliest followers shared that by putting our faith in Jesus, we are reconciled to God. All that is out of sync with God's purpose for our lives is forgiven, and we are restored to a right relationship with God.[198]

But it doesn't end there. The restoration of our relationship with God is just the beginning. God invites us to join him on his mission — representing Jesus as the present and future king of God's kingdom, a kingdom that arrived with Jesus' coming and will be fulfilled when he returns one day. Through the church's work, the world gets a glimpse — imperfect yet filled with promise — of the coming reign of God through Jesus. The church cares for the people that Jesus would care for, and challenges the people that Jesus would confront and challenge. In a very real sense, the church acts as Jesus' hands, feet, and mouth until he returns.[199]

## THE CHURCH EXISTS FOR OTHERS, NOT ITSELF

From the instant Jesus' church was birthed, it was about other people. Yes, the church first and foremost is worshipers of God. But "being the church" is so incredibly different from and more thrilling than merely "going to church." Recently, a group from my own church decided that they wanted to dedicate a day to bless and care for single mothers in our community. After contacting some local organizations, they were given the names of several single mothers, several of them homeless and living on the streets. They invited close to one hundred moms to our church building one Saturday, providing child care for them to give them a much-needed break. Our parking lot was transformed into an auto repair shop, and several of our church members volunteered to fix cars. Our gym became a hair salon, and several professional hairstylists came in to give free haircuts, coloring, and styling. The gym was redecorated with class, complete with comfortable couches and mirrors and flowers arranged throughout the room. Several rooms in our church building were set up to give massages as well, and we even provided free acupuncture. All of this was done by trained professionals. Two rooms were set up as a fashion boutique in which the moms got to pick out free clothing for themselves and their children. A professional photographer also was there to take family photos for them to have. They are planning to do another Day of Love (that's what they named it) in a couple of months.

I can't imagine that Jesus would not have been pleased with this way of representing him to these moms in need in our town.

Recently, a youth leader shared with me how a high school student had just prayed with him to follow Jesus. He was bursting with excitement as he described to me what happened. One of this student's friends had been praying for him for a long time, caring for him and building a relationship of mutual trust and respect. Eventually, this student began attending youth group meetings, getting to know some other students in the church. He began to sense God moving in his life, and he found he had faith to accept that what he was learning about Jesus was true. His high school friend, the one who had been praying for him for so long, was there to pray with him as he put his trust in Jesus. What this youth pastor was beaming about was that it wasn't him who shared Jesus and eventually prayed with this new Christian. It was the high school student who owned the mission himself.

Hearing stories like this is quite thrilling to me and brings me hope. Churches all across the world are doing some amazing things. People in churches aren't just "going to church"; they are being the church. That makes all the difference, because not only do Christians experience church the way it was meant to be, but very cool things happen as Christians serve other people in Jesus' name. The more this happens, the less the church will be thought of negatively. But it requires the church community to organize themselves collaboratively to serve others.

When Christians really act like Christ, people take notice.

## WE ARE DESIGNED FOR COMMUNITY AND DIVERSITY

It's interesting and sad when people say, "I don't need others. I can just be a follower of Jesus on my own." When they say that, it totally misses the beauty of being in a church. While it's true that each one of us, as individuals, are part of the church, the church, from the very beginning, has always been more than just a collection of casually connected individuals. The New Testament gives helpful instruction that the church should have some formal roles of leadership, accountability structures, regular practices and events like the celebration of baptism and the Lord's Supper, and regular meetings for worshiping together and caring for one another in community. We're not meant to function as Christians without being part of a church.

A healthy church is a community of creative diversity. We see this described in the Bible in a letter written by the apostle Paul. Paul uses the metaphor of the human body to describe how all the different parts of the church should work together.[200] Each person in the church is a different part of a single body, and we all need one another for the body to function the way God designed it to: "Now if the foot should say, 'Because I am not a hand, I do not belong to the body,' it would not for that reason cease to be part of the body. And if the ear should say, 'Because I am not an eye, I do not belong to the body,' it would not for that reason stop being part of the body. If the whole body were an eye, where would the sense of hearing be? If the whole body were an ear, where would the sense of smell be? But in fact God has placed the parts in the body, every one of them, just as he wanted them to be. If they were all one part, where would the body be? As it is, there are many parts, but one body."[201]

Paul reminds the church that being a follower of Jesus means that we each have a significant and meaningful place in the church, even though our gifts and passions are different. When you or I aren't there, serving with other believers in the unique and creative way God wants us to, the body isn't complete. You are part of keeping a body healthy and thriving. Never forget that! You haven't experienced the church as Jesus intended it to be until you are serving in a local organized body using your God-given giftedness on his mission. When you move from spectator to participant, your life will never the the same. No wonder so many are disillusioned by church, if that means waking up on Sunday to drive to a building for a sing-along and to hear a professional Bible person give advice on life, and then going home for another week. This isn't church. Please don't ever settle for merely "going to church." Talk to your church's leaders and ask how you can fit in and "be the church." I can guarantee you that most church leaders will gladly have you join in being the church with them.

## JESUS LOVES THE CHURCH, BUT HE ISN'T ALWAYS HAPPY WITH IT

When the church is functioning well and serving the world, it is a beautiful thing. Yet it isn't always so beautiful. The Bible makes it clear that while Jesus loves his church, he isn't always pleased with how his followers act. In various places in the Bible, we see that Jesus had some hard words for his disciples and for the churches that weren't following his teaching and representing him well. At one point, Jesus told a church that they had strayed so far from his teaching that he was about to spit them out of his mouth![202] Sometimes the church messes things up.

I've seen life-changing, life-altering, amazing stories of God using his church to help people in need and to represent Jesus well, and as a result people put faith in Jesus and follow him. I've also seen and experienced the messiness of the church when it strays from Jesus' teachings. But even through the mess we sometimes create, I have discovered there is great hope. There is a hidden beauty in the church, as God works through the broken lives of messy people.

# CHAPTER SEVENTEEN

# MESSY PEOPLE, MESSY CHURCH

★ ★ ★ ★

When we have been wounded by the Church, our temptation is to reject it. But when we reject the Church it becomes very hard for us to keep in touch with the living Christ. When we say, "I love Jesus, but I hate the Church," we end up losing not only the Church but Jesus too.

—*Henri Nouwen, Bread for the Journey*

**I'VE LONG BEEN A FAN** of a band called the Violent Femmes. They have this wonderful song called "Jesus Walking on the Water," and I've been at concerts where they start playing this song and the entire place erupts in communal singing. People start smiling, joyously singing the words to this upbeat hoedown:

Jesus walking on the water.
Sweet Jesus walking in the sky.
Sinking sand, took my hand,
raised me up, and brought me up.
I can hold my head up high.[203]

Often at these concerts a mosh pit develops, and there is usually some serious thrashing going on. For those who don't know what a mosh pit is, it's what happens when a group of people informally create a circle near the stage and dance. But the dancing in the mosh pit is more akin to pushing, with elbows flying and people slamming into each other. It's quite mesmerizing to watch, preferably from a balcony. Even though the dancing is aggressive and people sometimes get hurt, it's not because they are angry at each other. They do it because they enjoy moshing. I've seen people fall to the ground after getting slammed, only to have others help them back on their feet before they jump right back in.

At one Violent Femmes concert, there was a large and pretty intense mosh pit going. I am not a mosh pit person, so I was standing off to the side leaning against a wall when a large, buff shirtless guy, sweating profusely, pulled himself out of the mosh pit and stood next to me. I noticed he was bleeding above his eye, probably from a rough elbow. He didn't seem to notice, so I brought it to his attention. He gave me a fierce glare and wiped the blood from his cut, so I tried to avoid eye contact with him. I was beginning to feel a bit uneasy, but then the band started playing "Jesus Walking on the Water" and his whole countenance changed. He burst out singing, yelled "Jesus!" and with a big, happy grin ran right back into the mosh pit, singing about Jesus.

I've found that being in the church is, in some ways, like being in a mosh pit. We are all in it together and we all like the same music, so to speak. Most of the time, we're doing our best just to dance and enjoy being there, but still, there are times when people get hurt. Sometimes, the church gets it right and helps others get up when they fall. But at other times, people get stepped on while the rest keep dancing. Some people even get trampled in the confusion. It doesn't matter what size our church is — tiny, small, medium, large, mega, multimega — they all are messy.

> EVERY TIME CHRISTIANS POINT AT THE CHURCH AND SAY IT IS MESSED UP, WE POINT AT OURSELVES. WE ARE PART OF THE PROBLEM BECAUSE WE ARE THE CHURCH.

For those who say that we need to get back to the pure, New Testament house church model, we find that there were some big messes there as well. Just read the New Testament letter of First Corinthians and you'll find prejudice, sexual immorality among family members, drunkenness, pride, and false teaching. It can seem romantic to go back to another time and envision the church then as the perfect church, but the fact is the church has always been messy in all of its forms. We make mistakes because we are fallible human beings. Every time Christians point at the church and say it is messed up, we point at ourselves. *We* are part of the problem because *we* are the church.

## THE PAIN OF DISILLUSIONMENT WITH THE CHURCH

Several years after I became a Christian, I found myself working on the full-time staff of a church. After several years serving in youth ministry, I shifted to start a ministry for college students and people in their twenties. God blessed our efforts, and in a few years there were almost a thousand college students and young adults participating in the Sunday night meetings and smaller home groups we started.

The ministry was thriving and growing. And then everything fell apart.

Our ministry was attracting a lot of younger people who wouldn't normally attend a church. There were also many who had left the church and were coming back, giving church a second chance. We didn't change our theology or tamper with the core beliefs of the Christian faith; we simply experimented with and adjusted our methods and the values of our ministry to engage the culture and become more approachable to the people we were trying to reach.

Our Sunday night worship gatherings met in the same room as the rest of the church, but we redesigned the way the sanctuary was set up. We met in a large warehouse-like building, so we moved the chairs out of their straight rows and put them around some round tables, and we even set up some couches. We wanted to give it a more casual feel, more like a living room. To complement the verbal communication of the sermon with visual elements, we invited local artists to paint while I was teaching. We set up a coffeehouse in the sanctuary, something that was uncommon at the time. And we shifted our teaching and leading from the solo, senior-leader approach to more of a shared leadership style.

Theologically, our beliefs were the same as the rest of the

church, but outwardly we began looking very different from the rest of the church. It was all quite fun and exciting, but as we continued to grow, the senior leadership of our church became uncomfortable with some of these differences. Eventually, they decided it was time to make some changes so that our group looked a bit more like the rest of the church. They felt that what we were doing was just too different and didn't understand why we were doing things the way we were.

Eventually I was brought into an office for a meeting and was told that I needed to stop, disassemble the ministry, and make adjustments to conform the ministry to be like the rest of the church. It was surprising and more than a little ironic to hear all of this, because the things we were being asked to change were the very things we needed to do differently to connect with the twenty-somethings and college students who were now attending. I explained why it didn't make sense for us to do this, but it was useless. Since I wasn't involved in the upper leadership of the church, I had no choice but to follow their wishes.

## FLASHBACK TO THE CHRISTMAS MUSICAL AND FASHION JUDGMENTS

As all of this unfolded, the shock and emotional pain I experienced gave me flashbacks. It brought me back to the time when I hid behind the choir in a brown bedsheet wondering what I was doing there. It brought me back to the day I sat across from the pastor in his office and I was judged for my haircut and clothing. It brought me back to my time of questioning the church and anything organized. It felt like I lost my innocence and once again grew increasingly disillusioned with the church and the leadership. I fiercely struggled in my heart to trust those in leadership but found myself questioning their decisions. And it wasn't just this church I was disillusioned with; it was any church. I questioned the entire structure, culture, and traditions that were making it so hard for me to do what I felt God wanted us to do. The hurt I felt caused me to question the way leaders in the church use their power. I questioned the very idea of the organized church and went through some of the darkest days of my life.

What once was a joy to me, serving on the staff of the church, now was a wound. I was too discouraged even to spend time in the church office. I knew that unless something in my heart changed, I needed to leave the church, so I wrote a resignation letter and set up a meeting with the senior pastor. To me, this was more than just a decision to resign from that church. I was ready to give up on the church altogether, and I wanted to bag anything that had to do with organized Christianity.

As I was processing my emotions, preparing myself to turn in my resignation letter, I drove downtown to a comic book store to buy some new comics, something that I can escape into when I'm feeling stressed. Maybe it's a way of reverting to the comfort of my childhood, I don't know. When I got to the comic book store, I pulled into a parking spot on the street. I sat there in the car, praying, "God, why is this happening? I want to give up on church, God, because this is not what I was planning for. Is this really church, God? Or just leadership power and control?" I was at the point of giving up on church. Then I saw a girl in her early twenties walk between my car and the car parked right in front of me. I watched her cross the street and make her way down the block. And as I watched her, something profound happened to me.

## REMEMBERING THAT THE CHURCH IS NOT ABOUT ME

As this young woman walked down the street and disappeared in the crowd, I found myself wondering whether she was a Christian. I wondered if she understood the grace of God and the love of Jesus. I wondered if there were any Christians in her life, people who could break through any negative stereotypes she might have about Christianity and the church. As I was thinking about these things, I looked around at the dozens of people walking down the sidewalks. They had been there all the time, but I had not really paid much attention to them. But now I saw each one of them as someone incredibly loved by God, someone Jesus wanted me to care about. At that moment, I sensed God reminding me that all that was happening in my life wasn't just about me. God reminded me that the mission to love and serve people like that young girl was his mission. I remembered why I had gotten involved in the ministry in the first place.

It wasn't about me. It was about serving others.

I sat in my 1966 Ford Mustang on the street outside the comic book shop praying and sobbing for quite a while. I wish I could say that the gloom magically went away, but it didn't. What happened was that I felt a renewed confidence to make some decisions about how I was going to respond to what was happening to me. I realized that I didn't want to become a bitter person, as I had seen others do. I knew that I didn't want to be divisive, stirring up trouble and a spirit of disunity. I just wanted to follow Jesus and be part of creating his future church. Jesus loves people, and he loves his church. He chose the church to represent him and do his work in the world, even when it gets messy. My time in this specific church might be over, but I couldn't give up on church, because Jesus loves the church.

When I went to the leadership and told them that I couldn't serve at the church anymore, I was surprised that someone raised the idea of starting a *new* church, and I realized that God might still be at work, answering my prayers. Instead of resigning that day, I became involved in the leading and planning of an entirely new church, with the approval of our leaders, using the same philosophy and many of the same ideas that we had used in our college and young adult ministry. Several years later, we now have several worship gatherings on Sundays, and run a full-time coffeehouse, art gallery, and music venue in our church building. And I am thrilled to be serving in a local church community with so many people who desire to be the church together on a mission.

It would have been so easy to give up on the church at that point, but I am incredibly grateful that I didn't.

When you read the New Testament book of Acts, you find that there were many times when the leaders of the early church didn't see eye-to-eye.[204] Things didn't always go smoothly, and they frequently encountered opposition. Many were beaten, some were killed, while others were thrown in prison or had to travel long distances to do what God called them to do. Yet they didn't give up, despite the cost.[205] What kept them going? They were just so grateful to Jesus for loving and saving them, and they were passionate to share the good news about him with others.

Thankfully, my story had a happy ending. The leaders of our church blessed our new church and helped us in some significant ways. I realized that these people truly loved God, and I knew that they loved me, but we had very different ways of doing ministry, a different sense of what the church should look like. I realized that they weren't the problem, really. I saw that I am no different, that I am just as prone to make a mess of something God is doing. I could have lashed out, blaming others for the hurt they had caused, and become cold and bitter toward the church. Instead, God humbled me, opening my eyes to his love and mercy in my life and reminding me that we all have weaknesses and hurt others. What matters is that we stick around to help clean our messes up.

## THE BEAUTIFUL, MESSY CHURCH JESUS LOVES

In today's world, when a church or an individual Christian does something embarrassing, it certainly makes headlines quickly enough. But for all the wrongs committed in Jesus' name, there are many more acts of kindness, mercy, grace, and forgiveness that beautifully represent the name and the message of Jesus. Often, it's hard to see the beauty when the mess is what is highlighted and gets the attention. But it is all around us, if you look for it. I was recently in a church that was rallying their people to provide backpacks stuffed with school supplies for children whose families are in financial need. This may not get the same press as the moral failure of a prominent pastor, but if you stop to think about the hundreds of children who are helped by this simple act of service, you realize it's quite Jesus-like and beautiful.

That same morning, I got into a conversation with a young woman who had just placed her faith in Jesus. She was both excited and scared. I was able to share with her some of the same emotions I had felt when I first began exploring who Jesus is. She didn't grow up in a church, so it was all new for her. She told me that for the first time, she was beginning to understand just how much God loved her. She was starting to see how Jesus fit in and transformed her understanding of God. There were several people in that church involved in her life, walking with her on her journey of faith. She was learning from the Bible for the first time, and it was changing her life.

Right after talking with her, I had a conversation with someone who was coming out of an abusive situation and shared how the church had helped her get back on her feet. She was getting counseling through the church and her life was being changed.

I have seen churches build hospitals in poor countries, churches give hundreds of thousands of dollars to relief agencies and send volunteers to serve those in need, churches involved in efforts to stop sex trafficking and other forms of slavery. I could go on and on, sharing stories about the beautiful things the church is doing.

There are churches where people admit when they are wrong and ask for forgiveness when they make mistakes. These churches are still messy, but they also are communities of hope and healing. Today, we have a fresh opportunity, as does every generation, to be the church Jesus envisioned. We have the opportunity to align what we do with the teaching of the Scriptures and Jesus' mission. We can pray that God will help the church to be known for what we are *for* more than what we are against. We can become a people who are known more for our love, not for our judgmental attitudes or the ways we hurt each other.

## FORGIVING, AS JESUS FORGAVE US

Jesus said some beautiful words to his disciples as he was preparing them for his departure and explaining their new mission. He said, "A new command I give you: Love one another. As I have loved you, so you must love one another. By this everyone will know that you are my disciples, if you love one another."[206]

Jesus said that as his followers, we are to love each other as an outward sign to the world of our commitment to him. Love is an emotion, but it is also a choice we make. Though many have been disillusioned by their experiences with the church, I believe they have a very important role to play in its transformation. We learn from our mistakes, and as difficult as our experiences may be, God can use those for his good purposes to help others avoid what

### I DREAM OF A CHURCH . . .

Go to the Churchland page on **www.dankimball.com** to share stories of how the church has helped you in positive ways and express dreams of what the church could be. Let's focus on the beauty of the church and encourage one another with examples of the church being organized around the right things.

we have experienced. But it all starts with forgiveness. Author Henri Nouwen, writing about our need to forgive those who have wounded us, says this about forgiving the church:

> When we have been wounded by the Church, our temptation is to reject it. But when we reject the Church it becomes very hard for us to keep in touch with the living Christ. When we say, "I love Jesus, but I hate the Church," we end up losing not only the Church but Jesus too. The challenge is to forgive the Church.
>
> This challenge is especially great because the Church seldom asks us for forgiveness, at least not officially. But the Church as an often fallible human organization needs our forgiveness, while the Church as the living Christ among us continues to offer us forgiveness.
>
> It is important to think about the Church not as "over there" but as a community of struggling, weak people of whom we are part and in whom we meet our Lord and Redeemer.[207]

Nouwen reminds us that while the church, as a human institution, is fallible and often fails us, the church is also the presence of the living Jesus, a community of hope, love, light, and truth in the world. Despite our failures, Jesus continues to use broken vessels to serve his life-giving water to people. He still sends us out, fully aware of our flaws and failures, to represent him.[208] To experience Jesus' power, we must learn to forgive those who have hurt us and move forward in faith, knowing that Jesus is still the head of his body.[209] It won't be easy. There are no guarantees that people won't fail us again. But we must remember, in humility, that the mess we see in the church is because of people like me and like you, imperfect people who make mistakes.

I know of a pastor who was severely wounded by a church he served, and for some time afterward, he left the organized church. Recently, he got involved in a church again, and while he knows this church has some problems, he chooses to be there. He has come to realize that the church's mess is a means by which God shapes and refines us, helping us to grow and mature to become more like Jesus.

## LET'S NOT GIVE UP ON THE CHURCH

Our goal should not be to find the perfect church, one that is free from conflict and the problems that normally plague human relationships. Instead, we should ask, What mess will I choose to be in? And even more important, How might God use me to help clean up this mess? I know that some who are reading this have had bad and hurtful experiences in the church. But we can use those experiences to create positive church communities that avoid repeating ways we have been hurt. Whether it's in the church you're already in, or in another church, you are needed to help create the future church. I know there are some leaders who may never want to listen to new ideas or will never be open to change, but most pastors and church leaders would love to have you dream and serve with them to create the church that Jesus intended. God may be placing in you the very ideas and dreams that the leaders of your church would love to hear about and make happen.

# CHAPTER EIGHTEEN

# FROM CHURCHLAND TO GRACELAND

★ ★ ★ ★

> I will build my church, and the gates of Hades will not overcome it.
>
> — *Jesus (Matthew 16:18)*

**THE BIBLE TELLS US** about the time when Jesus was walking with his disciples and took them to a religious place. But it was not a place for Jewish worship; it was a location where the Greeks worshiped other gods, a place called Caesarea Philippi. This location was commonly called "the gates of Hades" and was a central location for the worship of the Greek god Pan. Pan typically was represented as a half-goat, half-man god of hunting and music, and he also was associated with fertility and sexuality. This place where Jesus brought his disciples was at the foot of a mountain, and there was a large cave there where spring water flowed out from beneath the stone.

The Greeks believed that the fertility gods lived in the underworld during the winter months and came up from beneath the earth in the spring. This cave was considered to be an entry place to the underworld, known to the Greeks as Hades. Some of the rituals they practiced included prostitution, and there was even sexual interaction between goats and human beings. Jesus' disciples must have been shocked, wondering what he was thinking bringing them there. Devout Jews avoided places like this at all costs, and it's likely many of the disciples felt extremely uncomfortable even walking near the shrine dedicated to Pan. It was highly unusual for a rabbi to bring his disciples to a place like this, because it was radically opposed to the worship of the God of Israel. So why did Jesus bring them there?

As they stood before the "gates of Hades," the entrance to the underworld, Jesus announced to his disciples the birth of his church. Jesus said to them, "I will build my church, and the gates of Hades will not overcome it."[210] I find it absolutely fascinating that Jesus chose to make his announcement of the birth of the church in a place where people went to worship other gods. He didn't choose a nice safe place where followers of God were meeting. He didn't go to the temple in Jerusalem to make his announcement. He chose a place where other gods were being worshiped, where horrible rituals and sacrifices were made every day. Jesus made a bold, visionary declaration: not even the gates of Hades would be able to resist God's purposes and the mission of the church.

Gates were a defensive structure, built to resist invaders. Jesus was saying, quite clearly, that the church would prevail against evil, injustice, and death. Nothing would be able to stop the church from bringing God's goodness and grace to people. From the very beginning, Jesus wanted his church to be defined by its engagement with the world. He did not want the church to be hidden away in a building somewhere, avoiding the evils of the world. Jesus didn't want his church defined by a once-a-week meeting in which people listened to a message and sang some songs. Jesus wanted his church to represent him right in the middle of the world, engaged with the surrounding culture.

This is why you see Jesus later praying, as he prepares for his death on a Roman cross, "My prayer is not that you take them out of the world but that you protect them from the evil one.... As you sent me into the world, I have sent them into the world."[211] Jesus prays that his followers won't just retreat into their own buildings or Christian subculture. He prays not that his Father would take them out of the world but that they, like him, would be sent into the world.

## THE CHURCH NEEDS YOU, AND YOU NEED THE CHURCH

There is a huge difference between sitting on the couch watching a football game on TV and actually playing the game on the field. On the couch, you are passive, watching from a distance. You eat potato chips and warm up a nice plate of nachos and drink some beer or soda. You watch the game and gain some calories doing it. Game after game, you sit and watch others in action. But if you are going to be playing in the game, your blood starts pumping faster and your adrenaline rushes as you prepare to go out on the field. You put on your shoulder pads and feel the strength of the protective gear on your body. You add some grease paint under your eyes, ready to engage the other team. You go out and work with your teammates toward the goal of winning the game. Muscles are stretched, calories are burned. You rely on your teammates, and they rely on you to play your position. You fulfill an important role on the team. (To be honest, I don't know what I'm talking about here. I bowl occasionally but have never once worn a uniform or played a serious game of football.)

Church is not a football game, but when the Bible describes the church's mission, it's clear that being the church is not about sitting back and enjoying the snacks that God provides while others play the game. Everyone is involved. And being a Christian is not a solo endeavor. We are on a team with other followers of Jesus, and each of us has a position to play. Without you, the team is not complete. It may function, but not the way it should.

If you can't relate to sports analogies, then think of yourself as part of an orchestra or a band with an instrument that God has gifted you to play. Without you, the orchestra or band is incomplete. Or think of yourself as a beautiful color that is missing from a painting. Without that color, the painting is incomplete. The Bible uses the Greek word *poema* to describe each of us as followers of Jesus. A *poema* is the product of a craftsman, a work of art or a beautiful poem, the fruit of creative labor. Paul writes that "we are God's handiwork [*poema*], created in Christ Jesus to do good works, which God prepared in advance for us to do."[212] Each and every Christian has been created by God in a unique way, like a piece of art or a poem. God custom-designed us for a purpose — doing good works that represent Jesus to others. The church is simply local groups of Jesus-followers, all serving together for a common purpose. Without your contribution, the church is missing something that only you can bring. It's important that you talk to the leaders in your church to see where you are gifted and how you can help with the mission of the church. If you are not yet aware of what your gifts are, most churches have classes or other ways for you to discover them. Don't be a spectator any longer; spectators don't experience church. Absolutely nothing compares with participating on the field or playing in the band. So many people have grown tired of church because they never experienced it the way the Bible describes it. The church needs you, and you need the church.

## FROM CHURCHLAND TO GRACELAND

Graceland is the name of the mansion that Elvis Presley lived in from the late 1950s until the day he died in 1977. Elvis didn't actually give it that name. It was called Graceland by the former owner, who named it after his daughter, a girl named Grace. When Elvis bought the house, he decided to keep the name.

I have visited Graceland several times, and it is quite an intriguing place. Each room showcases "the King," giving us glimpses into his life, his character, and his personality. But there is another Graceland I want to share with you, a place that has nothing to do with Elvis or his music. When you read through the Bible, you read about the incredible, amazing grace of God.[213] Grace is God's unmerited favor. Grace is love from God that seeks us out when we have nothing to give in return. Grace is God loving us when we are unlovable. Grace doesn't judge; grace loves. Grace isn't selfish; it is selfless. It is a kindness from God that we don't deserve. There is nothing we have done, nor can ever do, to earn this favor. Grace is a gift from God. I could write endless chapters about the grace of God. And when we grasp and receive this grace and trust in God's amazing grace, we can't help but live differently. This new way of living, this radically different experience of life, is what I call living in Graceland.

Graceland is not the same as Churchland. Churchland can unintentionally exclude people because of its various codes of approval, language, and values. Graceland, on the other hand, is all about including people to experience God's grace without having to be part of a nonbiblical manmade subculture. It's about being in a constant state of grace and appreciation, which results in our living in our culture, not creating a subculture, so we can share this incredible grace with others. The Bible says, "It is by grace you have been saved, through faith — and this is not from yourselves, it is the gift of God."[214] And this gift is one we so appreciate that we can't help but desire others to experience it as well. So we exist to serve Jesus by serving others and sharing the good news of grace with the world in our words and actions. This is Graceland, and that's where I want to live.

> **GRACE•LAND:**
>
> *n.* The beautiful, messy community of Jesus' followers, his church, who are so appreciative of and thankful for God's grace that they remain in the world, humbly sharing with others the wonderful news of Jesus and grace.

## GRACELAND ISN'T JUST ABOUT WHERE WE GO WHEN WE DIE

Out of an understandable concern, the subculture of Churchland puts a lot of focus on how being a Christian and putting faith in Jesus gets you to heaven when you die. Eternity is a long time, so of course we should be thinking about that. But in Graceland, the focus is on what happens in this life as we put faith in Jesus. It is confusing for people to hear about Jesus and be invited to become a Christian when they also encounter tracts that focus on heaven and hell. Now, most of these tracts were written with good intentions, but they subtly communicate that being a Christian mainly is about going to heaven and avoiding hell. I absolutely do believe there is a heaven and a hell, and that is a sobering truth, something we must never forget. Jesus himself often spoke about the reality of heaven and hell.[215] The problem is that in tracts like these, the primary message about what it means to be a Christian and why Jesus came is reduced to being only about what happens when we die. Often the explanation of what it means to be a Christian covers the following points:

> All people have sinned, which means they have not listened to or followed God's guidance (Romans 3:23).

The penalty for sin is death, which includes both our physical death and our spiritual death, our eternal separation from God (Romans 6:23).

Jesus Christ paid the penalty of sin, which refers to his substitutionary death on the cross, in our place, for our sins (Romans 5:8).

These tracts encourage us to repent, a process of turning our hearts and minds away from the direction that we are currently choosing and instead trusting Jesus and receiving what he has done for us. Is this all true? Again, yes. I affirm every word of it. I personally believe these three statements to be one hundred percent true, and what amazing truth it is!

But here is the problem: it doesn't end there with saying a prayer so you can go to heaven. That's just the beginning. After saying the prayer, we join in the bigger story that God has for us here in this life. I can see why for many Christians it can be disheartening over time if being a Christian simply means that we are now saved and are merely waiting to go to heaven when we die, trying to figure out how to manage our sins in the meantime. We "go to church" and let the paid professionals have all the fun while we watch. But this isn't the story of the Bible. This isn't what it means to be a Christian.

When we read the entire Bible and begin to understand the full drama of what God has done through Jesus, why the church exists, and the beautiful future God has for his people, it changes everything. I could write pages here trying to describe it for you, but thankfully there are some wonderful books and resources you can check out for more on this.[216]

The story we enter when we become Christians starts in Genesis chapter 1, not Genesis chapter 3. The story doesn't begin with the bad news about sin; it begins with blessing, goodness, and the beauty that God created.

## KNOWING THE WHOLE STORY AND OUR PLACE IN IT IS SO IMPORTANT

The Bible tells us the incredible story of how God created everything that exists, including human beings, whom he deeply loves. His plan was for human beings to coexist in this wonderful har-

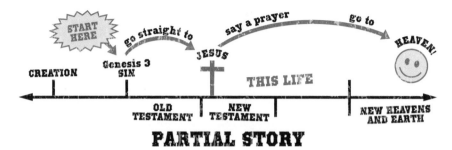

This story begins with how everyone is a sinner and needs Jesus. We pray the "sinner's prayer" so we are forgiven through Jesus and will go to heaven when we die. So for the rest of this life, we wait to be in heaven, "go to church," and manage our sin as best we can.

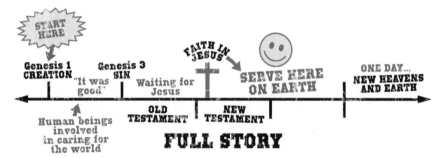

This story begins with creation and how God called human beings to steward the earth, and it was all good. But then sin entered the world. Consequently, we do pray for forgiveness and put our trust in Jesus as our Savior, but then we are immediately on a mission. Jesus came not so that we could escape to heaven but so that we could serve here on earth. We join God's work here through our sacred callings as parents, teachers, plumbers, lawyers, artists, or whatever God puts in our hearts as our vocation. One day we will be in eternal heaven, but we have a beautiful purpose and mission now.

mony of relationship with God and with each other, stewarding the earth for God. But the people he created thought they knew better than him, and they went against his guidance, upsetting everything — their relationships with God, each other, and the natural world. But because of his great love for them, God didn't abandon them to the consequences of their selfish choices. Instead, he chose a people group, Israel, to accomplish his plan of reconciling people to God.[217] The fulfillment of his plan was revealed when God himself was born as a man: Jesus. Jesus was concerned about people, healing them and caring for those who were neglected or marginalized by the culture. Jesus upset the staus quo, the normal way of doing things. Religious Jews didn't like him because he upset their religion, and the Roman leaders didn't like him because they saw him as a threat, a revolutionary. So they crucified him, executing him as a criminal, though he was guilty of no crime.[218] What those in power didn't realize was that something bigger than them was at work, that Jesus was taking on the penalty for their sins.[219] This was God's plan. In the person of Jesus, God showed us his great love, reconciling us to himself. Three days later, Jesus rose from the dead, demonstrating his victory over sin and death and confirming that everything he said and promised is true.

After he rose from the dead, Jesus appeared to hundreds of people and, after forty days, left this world to be in the presence of God. Jesus promised that God would send his Spirit to empower those who trust him, believing his words and putting their faith in him. When God sent the Spirit, the church was born. The Spirit enabled people to see their need for forgiveness, and by God's grace, through faith in Jesus and through what he did for us on the cross, we are reconciled to God.[220]

## THE STORY OF JESUS CONTINUES IN US

This is the story which we are invited into. This story is not like any other story. This story changes us from the inside out. As we put faith in Jesus, we are brought into the continuation of this story as the church.

The church is on a mission, representing Jesus and sharing with the world the good news about who he is and what he has done for us. As his followers, we care about the things Jesus cares about and do whatever we can to love people who are in need. We promote God's justice, standing against the unjust. We care for the oppressed. We take the incredible message of Jesus and bring it to the whole earth. The church exists as local communities that work together on a mission for Jesus, serving in the power of God's Spirit. The Bible teaches us that one day God will make all things new, and there will be a new heaven and a new earth, and that those who resist and reject the grace of Jesus will not be with him, that they will be removed from God's presence.[221] There is a great mystery in this, and it is beyond heartbreaking for me to think that some people will not fully experience God's love and grace for all eternity. But the joy of knowing Jesus, and thinking of those who don't know him, greatly motivates me to do whatever I possibly can in this life to share Jesus with others, to share not only about the reality of life after death but also about the incredible difference it makes knowing Jesus in the here and now. There is so much I want to let others know about: having peace with God, purpose, guidance, the grand narrative of where we come from and where we're going, having the forgiveness and love that come from God in amazing ways — things which I never understood before I became a Christian.

## ADVENTURES IN GRACELAND

As we've seen throughout this book, when you dig down below the surface, there are differences between how our culture views the church and how Jesus envisions it:

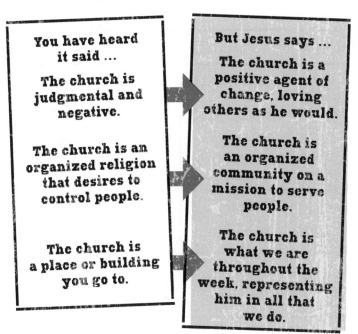

You have heard it said ...

The church is judgmental and negative.

The church is an organized religion that desires to control people.

The church is a place or building you go to.

But Jesus says ...

The church is a positive agent of change, loving others as he would.

The church is an organized community on a mission to serve people.

The church is what we are throughout the week, representing him in all that we do.

The urgent challenge for those of us who are part of the church is to better demonstrate with our lives who the Bible says Jesus is, and to work harder at correcting misperceptions about the church. This does not require any compromising whatsoever of the essential creeds or doctrines of Christianity.

We may need to offer an apology for the ways in which we, as a church, have strayed from our mission and have turned inward, becoming self-focused, critical citizens of Christian subculture. And we may need to offer an apology when the beautiful bride of Christ is used to serve a church leader's or a politician's agenda — or our own agendas — or when we have made messes and not cleaned them up. Even when we are not guilty of committing these wrongs, we still stand in as representatives of Jesus and his church.

We need to help turn Churchland into Graceland. If you are in a church, and you sense that it is one that might need to change, then perhaps God wants to use you to bring about that change.

| Churchland | Graceland |
| --- | --- |
| Focuses on what happens after we die | Focuses on what happens in this life |
| Counts decisions | Counts disciples |
| Begins the story of God and humans at Genesis 3 | Begins the story of God and humans at Genesis 1 |
| Full-time ministry and being on a mission is for paid church staff or those who go overseas | Full-time ministry and being on a mission is for all Christians, no matter where they live or what they do for a living |
| Tries to escape culture or creates Christian versions of culture | Immerses in culture and influences and creates |
| *Christian* is an adjective describing music and other things we label | *Christian* is a noun for people who live a certain way |
| Go to church | *Be* the church |

Begin by talking with your leaders to see how you can join in. Most of the church leaders I know would love to have mission-focused people helping them bring about any needed change to the church. Most church leaders are just working hard and trying to do their best to follow Jesus and love his people. In some cases, a church leader might not listen. If that happens, it might mean that God is moving you to another church that resonates with his mission. Just don't give up! The church needs you, and change sometimes isn't easy.

## DON'T MISS OUT

God has brought me on an interesting adventure, from drumming in a punk and rockabilly band in England, where I met an eighty-three-year-old pastor who broke my stereotypes about the church, to Israel, where I learned to depend on God, to California, where I got involved in the church. It wasn't easy as I experienced some difficult times in the messiness of organized religion, but I met Jesus in the mess. God used the organized church to change my life.

Although I don't know everyone who's reading this book, I hope that you'll consider the possibility that any negative experiences you've had with churches or Christians aren't representative of all churches and Christians. There is so much hope for the church, and the Jesus I met is someone I badly want you to know. Jesus is there in the messiness.

## STANDING AT THE GATES OF HADES

Several years ago, my wife and I visited Israel and Palestine. It was an opportunity for me to return to some of the places that had been so important in shaping my faith as a new believer in Jesus. (We didn't go to the Double Dough bread factory, though.) We chose to visit Caesarea Philippi — the place once known as the "gates of Hades," where Jesus announced the creation of his church. After arriving, we made our way from our car to the large rock base of the mountain. To this day, there is a small cave at the foot of the mountain, the very cave where people once believed that Pan and the gods of the underworld went in and out of Hades.

There are still niches carved in the rock walls where idols were once placed.

As we stood there, I opened my Bible to the book of Matthew and read the words that Jesus spoke in that very place to his disciples, centuries earlier: "On this rock I will build my church, and the gates of Hades will not overcome it."[222] My wife and I prayed in the cave, right in a niche that used to hold one of the idols of that time. We recommitted ourselves to a life on a mission with Jesus. We prayed that God would help us avoid the trap of Churchland and any form of status-quo Christianity or Christian subculture. We asked that God would place us smack in the middle of his mission, that he would help us to be part of a church that risks whatever is necessary to be the kind of church Jesus intended his church to be, and that we would break negative stereotypes about Christianity and the church.

My prayer today is that we all join together in this missional adventure that Jesus sent his original followers on. As much as we may hope for all people to follow Jesus and be part of his church, it won't be easy, because people don't always have positive experiences with Christians or the church. Let's not allow the church to get in the way of their encountering Jesus.

The great news is that we aren't alone in this mission. Jesus told us that we will be in community together and that the church is how he wants us to accomplish this mission. Everyone is needed — misfits and regular folks and all those God has gifted to join in this adventure of making Jesus and his grace known in this world. We are all in this together.

Welcome to Graceland.

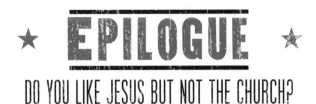

# ★ EPILOGUE ★

## DO YOU LIKE JESUS BUT NOT THE CHURCH?

**IN THIS BOOK,** I shared several stories about my adventures in trying to understand Churchland. Though many of the stories are about my life, I want you to know that I put these stories in to let you know about Jesus, how he has changed my life and the lives of all those who have chosen to follow him.

My adventures in Churchland are far from over, and in some ways it seems like they are just beginning. I wasn't able to fully address all of the questions I had about faith and the person of Jesus in this book. There were several other questions that I needed to answer. That's why I've written a follow-up book (tentatively titled *Do You Like Jesus but Not the Church?*). In this book, I address several more of the questions people have about Jesus and the beliefs of the Christian church, questions that intrigued and troubled me as a new follower of Jesus:

- Do we have to read all of the Bible literally? Is the Bible inspired, or is it a human document produced by ancient people and used by people today to promote their agendas?
- Is Christianity anti-gay?
- Is the Bible chauvinistic and oppressive toward women?
- Can I believe the Bible and still embrace science? Do I have to reject evolution to believe in the Bible story of creation?
- Does being a Christian mean you have to think that all of the other world religions are wrong?
- Is God a source of evil? Does the God of the Hebrew Bible promote war and violence, while the Jesus of the New Testament promotes peace?

- Why do many Christians focus so much on hell? Is hell real, or just something Christians use to scare people into believing?

These are important questions, ones I had to really look into as I was considering whether to trust Christianity and the church. I will address these questions in this follow-up book. You could think of it as "more adventures in Churchland."

I also welcome comments, both agreements and disagreements, and would love to interact with you on my blog about this book or about any questions you might have. A natural part of Christianity is thinking together, raising questions and learning from one another as we seek truth and study the teachings of Jesus and the Bible.

On www.dankimball.com you'll find a section about this book and a place to share your dreams for the church and encouraging stories of how the church has been a positive influence in your life. I love hearing other people's stories and experiences, because I do see us all as being on this adventure together, both in Churchland and in Graceland.

Jesus loves the church. Let's create the future church together.

# ★ NOTES ★

1. Mark 12:42 – 43; Luke 14:13 – 14; Matthew 22:39; 2 Corinthians 5:20.
2. Genesis 3; Romans 3:23; Romans 5:12; Romans 6:23; 1 John 3:4.
3. I highly recommend reading chapters 3 through 5 of the book *The Blue Parakeet: Rethinking How You Read the Bible* (Grand Rapids, Mich.: Zondervan, 2008) by my friend Scot McKnight. It's a great book about reading the Bible, and these three chapters wonderfully address the story line of the Bible.
4. Matthew 16:18.
5. Colossians 1:18.
6. Colossians 1:24; 1 Corinthians 12:27.
7. Matthew 16:18; Matthew 28:19 – 20; Acts 1:8 – 9.
8. Ephesians 5:22 – 23; Revelation 21:9 – 10.
9. Acts 4:13.
10. Dan Kimball, *They Like Jesus but Not the Church: Insights from Emerging Generations* (Grand Rapids, Mich.: Zondervan, 2007).
11. In the Easter musical later that year, Jesus appeared, freshly risen from the grave, in a similar plastic outfit. To this day, every time Easter comes around, I can't get that image of Jesus in the shiny white garbage bag out of my mind.
12. My rockabilly drummer heroes were men like D. J. Fontana (Elvis Presley's drummer), Jimmy Van Eaton (the original drummer for Jerry Lee Lewis who also drummed on many of the early Sun Studio recordings), and W. S. "Fluke" Holland (drummer for Carl Perkins and Johnny Cash). I also loved the neo-rockabilly and roots bands like the Stray

Cats, The Rockats, and The Blasters. I loved how these neo-rockabilly bands were able to bring the original rockabilly sound into the contemporary music scene.

13. The Christmas story is told in Matthew 1:18 – 2:18 and Luke 2:1 – 20. The Easter resurrection story is told in Matthew 26:17 – 28:20, Mark 14:12 – 16:9, Luke 22:7 – 24:52, and John 18:1 – 21:25.

14. Luke 1:46 – 55.

15. Matthew 1:20 – 24.

16. Matthew 2:16.

17. Luke 2:11.

18. Matthew 2:9 – 10.

19. D. R. W. Wood and I. H. Marshall, *New Bible Dictionary*, 3rd ed. (Downers Grove, Ill.: InterVarsity, 1996), 713.

20. KISS and Led Zeppelin were the very cool bands at the time. They still are cool, especially Led Zeppelin. Not sure about KISS anymore, though. Only two of the original four members are still in the band, so it's hard to think of them as still being KISS.

21. I use the term *Hebrew Bible* instead of Old Testament because calling it "Old," as it was later named, can subtly imply that it lacks relevance. Also, it can be insulting to religious Jews, who use only the "Old Testament" part of the Bible. You could call it "First Testament," which may be more appropriate. Because it was almost all originally written in Hebrew, I'll refer to it in this book as the Hebrew Bible.

22. Genesis 1; Psalm 19; Psalm 104; Job 38:4.

23. Psalm 111:10; Job 28:28; Proverbs 9:10; Proverbs 14:27; Proverbs 23:17 – 18.

24. *Miami Vice* was a popular '80s television show in which the main characters always wore light aqua blue and pink.

25. REM, "Shiny Happy People," *Out of Time* (Warner Brothers Records, 1991).

26. 1 Corinthians 11:23 – 26.

27. Mark later launched a successful blog and is an author and a magazine editor. He founded the blog *www.boingboing.net* and helped launch *Wired* magazine and *Make* magazine. He is a creative and intelligent thinker and a really good friend who helped shape my thinking.

28. Acts 17:11.
29. Incidentally, that's especially true when you are in church leadership. Often you hear church leaders talking about avoiding the evils of the world, but many of us turn around and consume McDonald's and Burger King cheeseburgers, neglecting the health of our own bodies.
30. Matthew 26:26 – 28.
31. Galatians 6:10.
32. J. David Cassal, "Defending the Cannibals," *Christian History.net*, January 1, 1998, *http://www.christianitytoday .com/ch/1998/issue57/57h012.html.*
33. Ibid.
34. Church leaders who are helping lead that change have written books about it, such as Francis Chan, *Crazy Love: Overwhelmed by a Relentless God* (Colorado Springs, Colo.: Cook, 2008); David Platt, *Radical: Taking Back Your Faith from the American Dream* (Sisters, Ore.: Multnomah, 2010); and Platt, *Radical Together: Unleashing the People of God for the Purpose of God* (Sisters, Ore.: Multnomah, 2011). These writers dream of a church that follows the teachings of Jesus and changes people's perceptions of the church.
35. Matthew 5:21, 27, 31.
36. I do address several more in the sequel to this book, tentatively titled *Do You Like Jesus but Not the Church?* See the epilogue for more information.
37. John 7:24.
38. 1 Samuel 16:7.
39. Dave Kinnamen and Gabe Lyons, *Unchristian: What a New Generation Thinks about Christianity* (Grand Rapids, Mich.: Baker, 2007).
40. Matthew 7:1.
41. Matthew 7:1.
42. John 7:24; John 8:15.
43. Matthew 7:1 – 5 TNIV.
44. Luke 18:9 – 14.
45. Matthew 7:2.
46. Matthew 7:15.
47. Matthew 7:6.

48. 1 Corinthians 5:1.
49. Leviticus 18:8; Acts 15:20, 29; Acts 21:25.
50. 1 Corinthians 5:2.
51. 1 Corinthians 5:3.
52. 1 Corinthians 5:2.
53. John 14:15.
54. John 14:23.
55. John 14:15 – 27; Acts 1:8; see also Romans 6 – 8.
56. 1 John 1:8 – 9.
57. Romans 6:1.
58. Acts 3:19.
59. Psalm 51:17; Psalm 66:2; Luke 19:11 – 32.
60. Ephesians 2:8 – 9.
61. 1 Corinthians 5:6.
62. 2 Corinthians 12:20; Ephesians 4:29 – 32; Proverbs 11:13; Proverbs 16:28.
63. 1 Corinthians 5:12.
64. Romans 3:9 – 26.
65. Colossians 4:5 – 6.
66. Romans 8:26.
67. Matthew 18:15 – 17.
68. Matthew 18:15 – 17.
69. Romans 3:23.
70. Galatians 6:1 – 2.
71. Galatians 5:22 – 23.
72. Colossians 3:12.
73. Romans 14:10 – 12; Revelation 20:11 – 15.
74. John 14:16; Acts 4:12; 1 Timothy 2:5; Acts 16:30 – 31.
75. *http://www.dankimball.com/vintage_faith/2009/11/how-would-you-define-organized-religion-.html*.
76. Hebrews 10:25.
77. A few extreme churches incorrectly take the verses in Mark 16:17 – 18 and Luke 10:19 to mean that you should bring poisonous snakes into worship gatherings.
78. For example, Acts 2:46; Romans 16:5; 1 Corinthians 16:19; Colossians 4:15.
79. 1 Corinthians 14:26.
80. Jude 12; 2 Peter 2:13; 1 Corinthians 11:17–34; Acts 20:7.
81. Jeanne Halgren Kilde, *When Church Became Theater: The*

*Transformation of Evangelical Architecture and Worship in Nineteenth-Century America* (New York: Oxford Univ. Press, 2002).

82. 1 Corinthians 11:20.
83. Hebrews 13:7, 17.
84. Ephesians 4:11 – 13.
85. From a sermon Nicky Gumble gave on evangelism at Alpha Conference in 2008.
86. Acts 2:46.
87. Acts 2:42 – 47.
88. Titus 1:5 – 9; 1 Timothy 3:1 – 13.
89. Matthew 5:44.
90. Matthew 22:39.
91. Mark 11:15 – 17.
92. Isaiah 56:7.
93. Jeremiah 7:11.
94. Matthew 22:21; John 18:36.
95. John 6:14 – 15.
96. John 2:19 – 20.
97. Isaiah 43:10; Isaiah 44:6, 8; John 17:3; 1 Corinthians 8:5 – 6; Galatians 4:8 – 9.
98. Matthew 3:16 – 17; Matthew 28:19; John 14:16 – 17; 2 Corinthians 13:14; Acts 2:32 – 33; John 10:30; John 17:11, 21; 1 Peter 1:2; Acts 5:3 – 4; 1 Corinthians 2:11 – 12; John 1:1, 14; John 10:30 – 33; John 20:28; Colossians 2:9; Philippians 2:5 – 8; Hebrews 1:8.
99. Genesis 1:1; Isaiah 44:24.
100. 1 Peter 2:24; Matthew 20:28; Mark 10:4.
101. James 1:27.
102. 1 Timothy 4:16.
103. John 4:1 – 26.
104. Acts 17:1 – 34.
105. Matthew 24; 1 Corinthians 15:23; 1 Thessalonians 4:13 – 18.
106. There are trusted Old Testament theologians such as John Walton from Wheaton College who propose some fascinating alternative takes on Genesis 1. See John Walton, *The Lost World of Genesis One* (Downers Grove, Ill.: InterVarsity, 2009).
107. Acts 17:10 – 12.

108. Daniel 1:1 – 8.
109. Mark 8:5; Matthew 13:10 – 17.
110. Galatians 6:10.
111. James 1:17.
112. Matthew 4:23; Matthew 13:54; Luke 2:39 – 52; Luke 4:16; John 7:14; John 10:23.
113. Matthew 26:17 – 30.
114. Colossians 2:23; Matthew 23:1 – 39.
115. Matthew 16; Acts 2.
116. 1 Corinthians 11:23 – 25; Matthew 28:19.
117. John 15.
118. 1 Corinthians 12:4 – 30.
119. Matthew 18:15 – 17; Titus 1:5 – 9; Ephesians 4:11 – 13.
120. Acts 6:1 – 7.
121. Acts 6:1 – 4; D. James Kennedy and Jerry Newcombe, *What If Jesus Had Never Been Born?* (Nashville: Thomas Nelson, 1994), 28.
122. Alvin J. Schmidt, *How Christianity Changed the World* (Grand Rapids, Mich.: Zondervan, 2004), 12.
123. The World Vision website is *www.worldvision.org*, and the Compassion International website is *www.compassion.com*.
124. My friend Rick McKinley and another good friend, Chris Seay, organized this church program. Resources are available at *www.adventconspiracy.org*.
125. You can find out more about the Not for Sale Campaign at *www.notforsalecampaign.org*.
126. Trade As One: *www.tradeasone.com*.
127. James 1:27; Matthew 25:44 – 45.
128. For example, Sam Harris, *Letter to a Christian Nation* (New York: Knopf, 2006).
129. R. J. Rummel, "Statistics of Democide: Genocide and Mass Murder Since 1900" (Charlottesville, Va.: Center for National Security Law, School of Law, University of Virginia, 1997), *www.hawaii.edu/powerkills/NOTE5.HTM*. See also Vox Day, *The Irrational Atheist: Dissecting the Unholy Trinity of Dawkins, Harris, and Hitchens* (Dallas: Benbella, 2008).
130. Day, *Irrational Atheist*, 97 – 111.
131. 2 Timothy 3:15 – 16.
132. 1 Corinthians 15:3 – 4; Romans 6:23.

133. Matthew chapters 5–7.
134. Hebrews 4:12.
135. 2 Timothy 3:16; Luke 1:1 – 4.
136. These were not to keep people inside. They were protective measures, because of ongoing Israeli-Palestinian tensions.
137. Guns N' Roses, "Welcome to the Jungle," *Appetite for Destruction* (Geffen Records, 1987).
138. There is less of this today, but it's still around.
139. John 17:15.
140. John 1:31; Matthew 7:28 – 29.
141. Matthew 9:36; Luke 19:41.
142. Luke 20:19 – 20.
143. John 21:25.
144. Genesis 1:27 – 31.
145. Romans 5:12 – 21.
146. Genesis 3:15.
147. Genesis 12.
148. 2 Samuel 7.
149. Isaiah 7:14.
150. Luke 1:27 – 37.
151. Isaiah 9:6 – 7; Luke 1:32.
152. Isaiah 9:1 – 2; Matthew 4:12 – 16.
153. Psalm 78:1 – 2; Matthew 13:34 – 35.
154. Isaiah 61:1 – 3; Luke 4:17 – 21.
155. Isaiah 53:1 – 4; Psalm 41:9; John 1:11; John 12:37 – 40; Luke 23:20 – 21; Isaiah 50:6; Matthew 27:26; Mark 14:40; Mark 15:15.
156. Psalm 22:15 – 17; Isaiah 52:14; Zechariah 12:9 – 10; Matthew 27:26 – 30; John 19:1 – 3, 33 – 35.
157. Matthew 4:2; Matthew 11:19; John 4:6; John 11:35; John 12:27.
158. Wayne Grudem, *Christian Beliefs: Twenty Basics Every Christian Should Know* (Grand Rapids, Mich.: Zondervan, 2005), 67.
159. Billy Graham, "Surviving in a World of Turmoil," *Decision Magazine*, July 1, 2003, *www.billygraham.org/articlepage .asp?articleid=329.*
160. Luke 2:11.
161. 1 Corinthians 7:9 – 10; Psalm 51:17.
162. Romans 3:23.

163. 1 Timothy 2:5; John 14:6; Acts 4:12.

164. Roman 6:23; Revelation 20:11 – 15; John 3:16.

165. Romans 3:24; 1 Peter 2:24.

166. 1 Corinthians 15:54 – 55; John 11:25.

167. Revelation 21:1 – 6; 2 Peter 3:13.

168. 1 Corinthians 15:3 – 8.

169. Matthew 28:18 – 20.

170. Acts 1:8.

171. John 17:15.

172. 1 Peter 4:5; Romans 14:9; 2 Timothy 4:1.

173. Revelation 19:16.

174. John 11:25 – 26.

175. John 6:44 – 47.

176. Luke 11:9; James 4:8.

177. The Altar Boys' lead singer and guitarist Mike Stand has a band called the Altar Billies, which, among other things, plays rockabilly versions of their earlier songs.

178. Peter McCabe and Jack Killion, "Interview with Johnny Cash," *Country Music*, May 1973, 53.

179. Patrick Carr, "Johnny Cash's Freedom," *Country Music*, April 1979, 54.

180. You can read Wanda's bio and learn more about her music on her website: *www.wandajackson.com*.

181. John 17:15.

182. John 17:15, 18.

183. Robert L. Saucy, *The Church in God's Program* (Chicago: Moody, 1972), 11.

184. W. D. Mounce, *Mounce's Complete Expository Dictionary of Old and New Testament Words* (Grand Rapids, Mich.: Zondervan, 2006), 110.

185. Genesis 28:10 – 12; Judges 19:18; 2 Samuel 12:20; 1 Kings 3:1; 2 Chronicles 3:3.

186. 1 Corinthians 3:16 – 17; Hebrews 3:6.

187. John 17:15 – 18.

188. 2 Corinthians 5:20.

189. Matthew 4:19.

190. Exodus 34:14; John 4:24; Romans 12:1 – 2.

191. Matthew 28:19 – 20.

192. Acts 1:7 – 8.

193. John 14:23 – 29.
194. For an excellent book about the Holy Spirit, I recommend Francis Chan, *Forgotten God: Reversing Our Tragic Neglect of the Holy Spirit* (Colorado Springs, Colo.: Cook, 2009).
195. Acts 2:1 – 40.
196. Acts 2:1 – 13.
197. 1 Kings 8:46; Psalm 14:3; Romans 3:23.
198. 2 Corinthians 5:18 – 20; Colossians 1:20 – 23.
199. Matthew 24:14; John 20:20.
200. 1 Corinthians 12:12 – 27.
201. 1 Corinthians 12:15 – 20.
202. Revelation 3:16.
203. Violent Femmes, "Jesus Walking on the Water," *Hallowed Ground* (Slash Records, 1985).
204. Acts 15:1 – 5; Galatians 2:11 – 16.
205. Acts 7:59; Acts 9:25; 2 Corinthians 11:32; Acts 12:2; Acts 23:12; Acts 28:30.
206. John 13:34 – 35.
207. Henri Nouwen, "Forgiving the Church," *Bread for the Journey: A Daybook of Wisdom and Faith* (San Francisco: HarperCollins, 1996), entry for October 27.
208. Matthew 28:19 – 20.
209. Matthew 16:13 – 17.
210. Matthew 16:18.
211. John 17:18.
212. Ephesians 2:10.
213. Ephesians 1:5 – 12; Ephesians 2:1 – 10; Nehemiah 9:17; Jonah 4:1 – 2; Titus 2:11.
214. Ephesians 2:8.
215. Luke 16:19 – 31; Matthew 18; and multiple other places.
216. The book *The King Jesus Gospel* by Scot McKnight (Grand Rapids, Mich.: Zondervan, 2011) goes into this in much detail, as does his book *The Blue Parakeet: Rethinking How You Read the Bible* (Grand Rapids, Mich.: Zondervan, 2008), which walks through the story line of the Bible.
217. Genesis 12:1 – 3; Genesis 3:14 – 16; Romans 11:25 – 27.
218. John 8:56 – 59; John 10:27 – 36.
219. Matthew 27:11 – 54; Romans 6:23.

220. John 16:8; Acts 2; 1 Corinthians 15:1–8.
221. 2 Thessalonians 1:9; Revelation 20; Revelation 21:1; Isaiah 65:17.
222. Matthew 16:18.